Series C
Pentecost I

Study Guide

By Ken Schurb
  and Richard Shuta
Edited by Thomas J. Doyle
  and Rodney Rathmann

SAINT LOUIS

Assistant to the editors: Cindi Crismon

The quotations from *Luther's Works* in this publication are from the American edition: vol. 31 copyright © 1957 by Augsburg Fortress, used by permission of the publisher.

Unless otherwise stated, the quotations from the Lutheran Confessions in this publication are from the BOOK OF CONCORD: THE CONFESSIONS OF THE EVANGELICAL LUTHERAN CHURCH, edited by Theodore G. Tappert, copyright © 1959 Fortress Press. Used by permission of Augsburg Fortress.

Scripture taken from THE HOLY BIBLE: NEW INTERNATIONAL VERSION ®. Copyright © 1973, 1978, 1984 by International Bible Society. Used by permission of Zondervan Publishing House. All rights reserved.

The "NIV" and "New International Version" trademarks are registered in the United States Patent and Trademark Office by International Bible Society. Use of either trademark requires the permission of the International Bible Society.

1   2   3   4   5   6   7   8   9   10   04   03   02   01   00   99   98   97   96   95

Contents

Introduction

About the Series

This course is 1 of 12 in the Church Year series. The Bible studies in this series are tied to the 3-year lectionary. These studies give participants the opportunity to explore the Old Testament lesson (or lesson from the book of Acts during the Easter season), the Epistle lesson, and the Gospel lesson appointed for each Sunday of the church year. Also, optional studies give participants the opportunity to study in depth the lessons appointed for festivals that fall on days other than Sunday (e.g., Ascension, Reformation, Christmas Eve, Christmas, Epiphany, Maundy Thursday, Good Friday).

Book 1 for years A, B, and C in the lectionary cycle will include 17 studies for the lessons appointed for the Sundays and festival days in Advent, Christmas, and Epiphany. Book 2 will include 17 studies for the lessons appointed for the Sundays and festival days in Lent and Easter—and for Ascension and Pentecost. Book 3 (15 sessions) and 4 (16 sessions) for years A, B, and C will include studies that focus on the lessons appointed for the Pentecost season.

After a brief review and textual study of the Scripture lessons appointed for a Sunday or festival day, each study is designed to help participants draw conclusions about the individual lessons, compare and contrast them, discover a unifying theme in them (if possible), and apply the theme to their lives. At the end of each study, the Scripture lessons for the next Sunday and/or festival day are assigned in preparation for the next session. The Leaders Guide for each course provides additional information on the appointed lessons, answers to the questions in the Study Guide, a suggested process for teaching the study, and devotional or worship activities tied to the theme.

May the Holy Spirit richly bless you as you study God's Word!

Session 1

The Holy Trinity, the First Sunday after Pentecost

Proverbs 8:22–31; Romans 5:1–5; John 16:12–15

Focus

Theme: *Not Alone*

Law/Gospel Focus

We are totally unable to recognize the Father's unmerited love except through the Lord Jesus Christ, who reflects to us the Father's loving heart. Luther says it well: "Without Christ we see nothing in God but an angry and terrible Judge. But we could know nothing of Christ, either, if it were not revealed to us by the Holy Spirit" (F. Samuel Janzow, *Getting into Luther's Large Catechism* [St. Louis: CPH, 1978], p. 93).

Objectives

That by the enabling power of the Holy Spirit working through God's Word we will
1. identify what Scripture says about all our Triune God's works for us: creation, redemption, and sanctification;
2. confess confidently that God in three Persons does not leave us in our loneliness;
3. help and befriend others as we share with them the blessings the Triune God so freely gives to us.

Opening Worship

Pray together the prayer "For Those Who Are Lonely" (*LW*, p. 132).

Almighty God, merciful Father, by Word and Sacrament You have created Your Church in this world to be a godly communion and family. Grant Your blessing to those who dwell in loneliness that they may find a place of solace and pleasant fellowship among people faithful to You; through Jesus Christ, our Lord. Amen.

Introduction

1. When do you feel most lonely? Pick one or more situations from the list below, or add your own.
   - At home alone
   - On a long business trip
   - At a social gathering where you know few others
   - At an airport
   - At work or school
   - When you're cheering in the minority at a sporting event
   - With a particular person
   - Other
2. Why is loneliness uncomfortable?

3. React to the statement, "Sin is the road to loneliness." How can sin lead to loneliness?

Inform

The three lessons for our study tell us how the one God, Father, Son, and Holy Spirit in an eternal community of love, invites us into fellowship with that love.

The Old Testament lesson from Proverbs 8 forms a high point of the Bible's wisdom literature (Job, some of the Psalms, Proverbs, Ecclesiastes, and Song of Solomon). This text shows Wisdom as more than just a quality God has or a gift He gives. Here we meet Wisdom as a Person, the One in whom the Lord delighted from eternity and with whom God created the universe. In short, this "Wisdom" is none other than the Second Person of the Trinity, the Son of God, before He became the man Jesus of Nazareth.

1. For present purposes there are two important points to note about Christ in this passage. One of them comes in verses 24–30a. Summarize it.

b. The other big point about "Wisdom" is found in verses 30b–31a. Summarize it.

c. Put these two points together into one summary statement.

2. God created us for the very purpose that He might redeem us and make us holy. How does this statement relate to what you have learned from Proverbs 8?

3. The Epistle lesson follows the section on justification by grace for Christ's sake through faith in Romans 3:21–4:25. Now Paul emphasizes the divine Judge's acquittal of the guilty, with application to Christian life, in a passage which features all three Persons of the Trinity.
Write a brief summary of what the passage says about
a. the Father;

b. the Son;

c. the Holy Spirit.

4. Now, write a statement that reflects the work of the Trinity.

5. Besides giving and entrusting to us everything in heaven and earth, God has given us His only Son and His Holy Spirit in order to bring us to Himself through them. How does this point relate to your life?

6. The Gospel lesson records Jesus' words spoken on the night before His crucifixion.
   Write a brief summary of what Jesus said about
   a. the Father;

   b. the Son;

   c. the Holy Spirit.

7. Now, write a statement that summarizes what Jesus says about Himself, the Father, and the Holy Spirit.

    Sinners are totally unable to recognize the Father's favor except through Christ, who is the mirroring image of the Father's heart. Without Him we behold God as an angry and terrible Judge. But we could know nothing of Christ were He not revealed to us by the Holy Spirit.

8. Review the three lessons and list some facts you have learned about the Holy Trinity.

Connect

    When our original parents chose to believe and act on the twisted words of the serpent, they found themselves alone and lonely. Similarly, the serpent continues to lie to us about relationships. What are some of Satan's lies? Here are some of the most common:

- As long as no one finds out what I am really like, I won't be lonely.
- If I pretend I'm not lonely, the loneliness I feel will go away.
- As long as my established relationships don't change, I won't be lonely.
- If I'm successful, I won't be lonely.
- If I please others, I won't be lonely.

1. Which of these has Satan spoken to you? Can you think of others he has spoken to you?

2. How does what you have learned about the Trinity—Father, Son and Holy Spirit—provide you with comfort and hope as you hear Satan's lies and are tempted to believe them?

3. Our wonderful God—Father, Son and Holy Spirit—created us for relationship with Him and others. When we broke the relationship He had established between Himself and us, the Father sent His Son to reconcile all people to Himself and restore the original relationship. The Holy Spirit continues to strengthen and preserve that relationship as He works through Word and Sacrament. By His grace through faith He offers us oneness with Him, wholeness within ourselves, and encouragement and love from others. The eternal relationship He established for us with Him through His Son's death on a cross provides us the enabling power to resist Satan's tempting lies, forgiveness when we believe Satan's lies, and rootedness in a relationship in which we affirm His constant presence in our lives.

    Remembering God's great love, what might you do as the cloud of loneliness looms over you? Share your thoughts with a partner.

Vision

During This Week

1. Sing some of the church's great hymns for the Holy Trinity, rejoicing that from all eternity God has known and shown how to love and share.
2. Reflect on these words from Luther:
   "A Christian lives not in himself, but in Christ and in his neighbor. Otherwise he is not a Christian. He lives in Christ through faith, and in his neighbor through love. By faith he is caught up beyond himself into God. By love he descends beneath himself into his neighbor" ("The Freedom of a Christian." [Luther's Works, 31: 371].)
3. Seek at least one way to put Luther's words into practice.

Closing Worship

Pray or sing stanzas 2 and 5 of "Jesus, I My Cross Have Taken" (*TLH* 423).

> Let the world despise and leave me,
> They have left my Savior too.
> Human hearts and looks deceive me;
> Thou art not, like them, untrue.
> And while Thou shalt smile upon me,
> God of wisdom, love and might,
> Foes may hate and friends may shun me;
> Show Thy face, and all is bright.
>
> Take, my soul, thy full salvation;
> Rise o'er sin and fear and care;
> Joy to find in every station,
> Something still to do or bear.
> Think what Spirit dwells within thee,
> What a Father's smile is thine,
> What a Savior died to win thee;
> Child of heaven, shouldst thou repine?

Scripture Lessons for Next Sunday

Read in preparation for the Second Sunday after Pentecost 1 Kings 8:22–23, 27–30, 41–43; Galatians 1:1–10; and Luke 7:1–10.

Session 2

The Second Sunday after Pentecost

1 Kings 8:22–23, 27–30, 41–43; Galatians 1:1–10;
Luke 7:1–10

Focus

Theme: *The Blessedness of Receiving*

Law/Gospel Focus

Before God, we sinners remain beggars who can only receive what He gives in His grace on account of Christ. We are all "poor in spirit." As the hymn writer says, "Nothing in my hand I bring; simply to Thy cross I cling." God in Christ abundantly blesses us with a continual outpouring of His rich goodness, which comes to us by way of Calvary's cross.

Objectives

That by the enabling power of the Holy Spirit working through God's Word we might
1. recognize that, for the Christian, to *believe* is to *receive*;
2. become satisfied receivers, in faith, of all the riches God gives us on account of Christ.

Opening Worship

Sing or pray together the stanzas 1 and 3 of the hymn, "Rock of Ages" (*LW* 361).

> Rock of Ages, cleft for me,
> Let me hide myself in Thee;
> Let the water and the blood,
> From Thy riven side which flowed,
> Be of sin the double cure:
> Cleanse me from its guilt and pow'r.

Nothing in my hand I bring;
Simply to Thy cross I cling.
Naked, come to Thee for dress;
Helpless, look to Thee for grace;
Foul, I to the fountain fly;
Wash me, Savior, or I die.

Introduction

1. On a scale of 10—strong, to 1—weak, how would you describe your faith in Jesus? Explain your response.
2. What do you use to measure your faith in Jesus? Check all that apply.
   • my feelings
   • my attitude
   • my actions
   • others' attitude toward me
   • other

When thinking about our faith in Jesus we tend to fix on the great feelings that faith had led us to experience, or the fine works that it leads us to do. Such things are good and important in the proper perspective, that is, when set against the backdrop of God's unmerited mercy. The most important thing about faith is that it receives Christ and His blood-bought forgiveness. Luther expressed the same idea when he characterized faith's first function as simply opening up a sack into which God pours blessings. We can only describe or measure our faith in Jesus by God's abundant grace that led Him to send His only Son into this world to live, die, and rise again for us. Together, today's Scripture lessons underscore for us the blessedness of receiving.

Inform

1 Kings 8:22–23, 27–30, and 41–43 are excerpts from Solomon's prayer at the dedication of the temple in Jerusalem. Verses 22–23 contain the beginning of the prayer; verses 27–30 ask the Lord to hear the prayers offered by Israel and her spiritual leaders at the temple

from that day forward; and verses 41–43 anticipate prayers which would be offered at the temple by Gentiles, namely, people who would travel to Israel and take up residence there.

Galatians 1:1–10 contains Paul's theologically packed greeting to the Galatian Christians as well as his initial thrust against the Judaizers who were turning the Galatians aside from the genuine Gospel to salvation by keeping the Law.

Luke 7:1–10 (parallel in Matthew 8:5–13) describes Jesus' conversation (through proxies) with a Roman centurion who had a deathly sick slave. Jesus comments on the centurion's remarkable faith and heals the servant without having to go to the centurion's home.

Answer the following questions:

1. What did God give in each lesson?
   a. 1 Kings 8:22–23, 27–30, 41–43

   b. Galatians 1:1–10

   c. Luke 7:1–10

2. What did people receive in each lesson?
   a. 1 Kings 8:22–23, 27–30, 41–43

   b. Galatians 1:1–10

c. Luke 7:1–10

3. How does each lesson show the importance of receiving what the Lord gives as He gives it (that is, not necessarily as we would like to have it)?
   a. 1 Kings 8:22–23, 27–30, 41–43

   b. Galatians 1:1–10

   c. Luke 7:1–10

Connect

1. In one of the confessional documents, the Apology of the Augsburg Confession, we learn:
   "The service and worship of the Gospel is to receive good things from God, while the worship of the law is to offer and present our goods to God. We cannot offer anything to God unless we have first been reconciled and reborn" (Ap IV 310).
   Which do you tend to emphasize in your own thoughts about God and your faith in Jesus—the service and worship of the law, or that of the Gospel? Explain.

2. How might you respond to each of the following comments:
   "I feel so distant from God."

   "If I tried harder to be a good person I would have a stronger faith."

   "I have accepted Jesus into my heart."

3. Based upon what you have learned about your faith from your study of Scripture, how can you be assured of your faith?

4. We respond to that which we have received in abundance from Him—faith—by bearing fruit (Galatians 5:22–23). How does the fruit we share demonstrate the abundance of faith with which God has blessed us?

========= **Vision** =========

During This Week

1. Dr. Dale Meyer of "The Lutheran Hour" notes that when we take time for God to speak to us in daily, quiet meditation and devotion through His Word, God helps us to live our theology. True, these times may seem to be unproductive because we are not *doing* anything in those minutes or hours. But that is precisely the idea: "nothing in my hand I bring; simply to Thy cross I cling." Live your theology by being filled from God's abundance of Gospel blessings. Take time to receive from God in His Word.

2. Respond to this statement "Christianity is a religion of gratitude."

Closing Worship

Sing or pray together stanza 1 of "By Grace I'm Saved" (*LW* 351)
By grace I'm saved, grace free and boundless;
My soul, believe and doubt it not.
Why stagger at this word of promise?
Has Scripture ever falsehood taught?
No; then this word must true remain:
By grace you too will life obtain.

Scripture Lessons for Next Sunday

Read in preparation for the Third Sunday after Pentecost 1 Kings 17:17–24; Galatians 1:11–24; Luke 7:11–17.

Session 3

The Third Sunday after Pentecost

1 Kings 17:17–24; Galatians 1:11–24; Luke 7:11–17

Focus

Theme: *In the Midst of Death, Christ Calls Us to Life*

Law/Gospel Focus

Death daily surrounds us in ways great and small, but our Lord intervenes for us with His strong Word of forgiveness and eternal life.

Objectives

That by the enabling power of the Holy Spirit working through God's Word we might

1. acknowledge our helplessness in sin, which always pays its wage—death;
2. find comfort in Christ, who by His Word of grace continues to intervene in our hopeless condition;
3. rejoice now and forever in the living Christ, who brings forgiveness and life from His cross and empty tomb.

Opening Worship

Pray Psalm 90 responsively.

Leader: Lord You have been our dwelling place throughout all generations.

Participants: Before the mountains were born or You brought forth the earth and the world, from everlasting to everlasting, You are God.

Leader: You turn men back to dust, saying, "Return to dust, O sons of men."

Participants: For a thousand years in Your sight are like a day that has just gone by, or like a watch in the night.

Leader: You sweep men away in the sleep of death; they are like the new grass of the morning—though in the morning it springs up new, by evening it is dry and withered.

Participants: We are consumed by Your anger and terrified by Your indignation.

Leader: You have set our iniquities before You, our secret sins in the light of Your presence.

Participants: All our days pass away under Your wrath; we finish our years with a moan.

Leader: The length of our days is seventy years—or eighty, if we have the strength; yet their span is but trouble and sorrow, for they quickly pass, and we fly away.

Participants: Who knows the power of Your anger? For Your wrath is as great as the fear that is due You.

Leader: Teach us to number our days aright, that we may gain a heart of wisdom.

Participants: Relent, O Lord! How long will it be? Have compassion on Your servants.

Leader: Satisfy us in the morning with Your unfailing love, that we may sing for joy and be glad all our days.

Participants: Make us glad for as many days as You have afflicted us, for as many years as we have seen trouble.

Leader: May Your deeds be shown to Your servants, Your splendor to their children.

All: May the favor of the Lord our God rest upon us; establish the work of our hands for us—yes, establish the work of our hands.

Introduction

As Psalm 90 and two of the lessons for this Sunday tell us, death is a present reality. We must come to terms with it. In fact, all people would spend their lives in crisis over their mortality except that everyone finds ways to cope.

1. List some ways in which the world tries to cope with death.

2. List some ways in which death, the cruel intruder, makes its reality felt in spite of our attempts to cope.

3. Note this statement: "Death begins to 'kill' us already before it actually comes. It robs us of our enjoyment of life, for we know that it will strike sooner or later." Do you agree or disagree? Why?

The Living Lord has Good News for us! He Himself intervened in the midst of our death-ridden condition to bring us life. This point is made in each of our three Scripture lessons.

==== **Inform** ====

1 Kings 17:17–24—Through Elijah, the Lord restores to life the son of the widow with whom Elijah stayed at Zarephath during a great drought. "Now I know that you are a man of God and that the word of the LORD from your mouth is the truth," the widow tells Elijah (v. 24).

Galatians 1:11–24—Paul answers an attack on his apostolic authority by emphasizing that his message came directly to him from Christ, and not from any mere secondary human source.

Luke 7:11–17—Jesus interrupts a funeral procession and raises the son of a widow at Nain in Galilee.

Study 1 Kings 17:17–24 together with Luke 7:11–17. Answer these questions.

1. What features do these two accounts have in common?

2. How do these accounts differ from each other?

3. What do these accounts tell you about what our Lord does about death, and how He does it?

Connect

The readings from 1 Kings and Luke both point to the truth and power of God's Word. So does the Epistle lesson from Galatians 1. In fact, Paul writes to the Galatians about death, too—the living death from which Christ freed him, and the death with which the Judaizers were trying to enslave the Galatians as they insisted that Christians must obey the law of Moses in order to be saved.

We are told in all three texts that the only thing that can fight death is the strong and gracious Word of Christ. To help you understand Galatians 1:11–24 and its context, read the story below.

Sherlock Holmes watched as Jude A. I. Zer, bureau manager of Church, Inc., screamed, "Hypocrite!" at Paul d'Apostle. Zer had hired Holmes to investigate d'Apostle on in-house charges of fraudulent claims.

Softening his tone, Zer went on, "I mean, at some time all of us have not lived consistently with the firm's high standards. That's a prime concern of mine. Perhaps you've gotten carried away with this 'grace' concept."

d'Apostle responded, "I'm not a weak link within the firm, although once I had been an opponent outside it. In fact, I openly tried to destroy it. *Your* treachery sickens me because it's a prettied-up version of what I was doing."

"WHAT?" Zer raged again. "The nerve! By your own admission, you have not been with the firm from its beginning. What gives a scum like you ..."

"The Founder," d'Apostle said evenly. "Sure, I was a scum, and I still am. Back then I wouldn't have admitted as much, but now I do—because the Founder let me in on His plan. I learned what He invested to start this firm. He showed me how His investment paid off, too, unlike my speculations. And, it turns out, He'd had His eye on me.

Not only would He cut me in on the action, free of charge; He also wanted me to represent Him and offer this deal to strangers."

"This is absurd," Zer told Holmes. "Ask any member of my staff …"

"Talk to as many staff members as you like," d'Apostle said. "I've got the word straight from the top."

"And you did not consult anyone else, Mr. d'Apostle?" Holmes asked.

"No," d'Apostle said. "I spent three years in a place where nary a person had heard of the firm. Only then did I visit members of the board."

"Ah yes, the board," Zer interjected. "My colleagues and I have long-standing, affectionate ties with its members. And what do you have?

"Virtually nothing," responded d'Apostle. "That's my point. I stopped by the home office for a visit, but I only saw two board members."

"And you didn't try to get them to vouch for your activities?" asked Zer.

"The subject didn't come up. Ask them." d'Apostle continued, "Then I traveled far from the home office, working for years in a new place. By the way, people received me very well there, even though they knew my background."

Holmes concluded the interrogation. The next day he announced his findings to Zer, with d'Apostle present: "d'Apostle is telling the truth."

Zer had to sit down. He stammered, "But my colleagues and I— our professionalism—our long-standing connections and business sense—and it's our word against his! How could you conclude that he is right and we're wrong?"

"Most elementary; in fact, a simple case of elimination," said Holmes. "I've checked out d'Apostle. He consulted no one. Either his story is sheer fabrication—unlikely, since he has a stake in the venture too—or he *has* had an audience with the Founder. No opportunity, no motive; ergo, no crime. So Mr. Zer, I would not want to be in your shoes when you meet your Founder."

Turning to d'Apostle, Holmes went on, "Now, my good fellow, please do not start to think that I approve of your ideas. I am a businessman myself, and I agree with Zer that simply giving your product away shows poor business sense."

d'Apostle said, "Holmes, your argument is not with me, but rather with the Founder. By the way, I'd hate to be in *your* shoes when you meet Him."

"Yes," Holmes mustered, "quite."

Discuss the story and Galatians 1:11–24. Use the following questions.
1. How do the characters (except, of course, Sherlock Holmes) and their actions in the story correspond to those in Galatians 1:11–24?

2. In defending himself against the Judaizers, Paul was defending the truth that the Law can only lead to death and that only the Gospel has the power to give life—abundant and eternal. Why does Paul defend the true faith with such zeal? Why is it so important for us to defend the teachings of God's Word?

3. In effect, Paul told the Galatians that he had the Word from the top. So do we. What comfort does this give you as you face or contemplate death?

Vision

During This Week
1. Write a note of Christian encouragement to someone who has recently experienced the death of a loved one.
2. Remind yourself daily that you have the Word from the top that defeats death. Sing several Easter hymns, alone or with family members. (They're never out of season!)

Closing Worship
After a western eye doctor performed successful surgery on a Mid-

dle Eastern king, he faced a problem: how much to charge the king? Charging too little would be taken as an insult. On the other hand, the king would likely be angered if the bill ran too high. So the doctor sent the king a note: "The king can do no wrong." The next day, the king's messenger brought the note back along with a check for a huge sum, much more than the doctor would ever have charged. The doctor was glad that he had left it to the king.

When we meet with various symptoms of death, leaving matters to our King may not seem greatly comforting. Here God's powerful Word about death and resurrection in Christ can be of supreme help to us. It assures us in the strongest possible way that the King is not playing cruel tricks on us.

But this good and authoritative Word does more than tell us God's intentions. It also unleashes in our lives the same power to raise the dead which we have seen in Scripture today. The Good News of Christ enables us to say, loudly and with confidence, "the King can do no wrong." On account of Christ, our King means to do nothing but right for us.

Let us pray:

Lord Jesus, who died for us: You can do no wrong. Speak to us with Your own forgiving Word of power and authority, and cause us to live, even as You live and reign with the Father and the Holy Spirit forever. Amen.

Scripture Lessons for Next Sunday

Read in preparation for the Fourth Sunday after Pentecost 2 Samuel 11:26–12:10, 13–15; Galatians 2:11–21; Luke 7:36–50.

Session 4

The Fourth Sunday
after Pentecost

2 Samuel 11:26–12:10, 13–15; Galatians 2:11–21;
Luke 7:36–50

Focus

Theme: *How God Handles the Self-Righteous*

Law/Gospel Focus

We do not want to subject ourselves to the same standards which we apply to others. Despite our guilt, God judges us "not guilty" on the basis of what Jesus Christ has accomplished for us.

Objectives

That by the enabling power of the Holy Spirit working through God's Word we might
1. apply God's Word of Law and Gospel to ourselves in the midst of our self-righteousness;
2. value the extravagance of God's forgiving love toward us in Christ;
3. keep in touch with the Savior and His bountiful Gospel goodness.

Opening Worship

Sing or pray together stanzas 3 and 4 of "Salvation unto Us Has Come" (*LW* 355).

> It was a false, misleading dream
> That God His Law had given
> That sinners could themselves redeem
> And by their works gain heaven.
> The Law is but a mirror bright

To bring the inbred sin to light
That lurks within our nature.

Since Christ has full atonement made
And brought to us salvation,
Each Christian therefore may be glad
And build on this foundation.
Your grace alone, dear Lord, I plead,
Your death is now my life indeed,
For You have paid my ransom.

Introduction

Work together to make two lists. On list 1 note traits of personality and behavior that you find undesirable in others. For list 2 mention some of your own traits that you know are irritating to others if you are comfortable doing so. Take only 15 seconds to collect your thoughts for each list, and allow only 1 minute for group members to call out items while someone writes them on chalkboard or newsprint.

When do the comparisons we make between ourselves and others become roads to self-righteousness? Why do we so easily take these detours? Why do we often not want to be subject to the same standards we wish to see applied to others?

There is no more level ground than found at the foot of the cross. We learn this in each of our three Scripture lessons.

Inform

Here are a few notes on the lessons for this Sunday:

The Old Testament lesson, 2 Samuel 11:26–12:10, 13–15, comes in the wake of King David's adultery, with Bathsheba. To hide his sin, David has murdered Bathsheba's husband, Uriah. The details are in 2 Samuel 11. For insight into David's spiritual state before and after his talk with Nathan, see Psalms 51 and Psalm 32.

The Epistle, Galatians 2:11–21, concerns the apostle Peter's behavior in Antioch, a city which served as a launching pad for missions to the Gentile world in the first-century church. Peter had been eating with Gentiles there (no doubt recalling the lesson God had taught him in Acts 10) until representatives of the Jerusalem congregation ("certain men from James") arrived, at which point he ceased to do so. Eating with the Gentiles was an important matter. First, it demonstrated that Peter recognized Gentile Christians in fellowship with Christ, himself, and the other Christians from Jewish backgrounds. Also, during such eating with Gentiles no effort would likely have been made to conform to Old Testament dietary laws (which are not binding for New Testament Christians, Mark 7:18–19; Acts 10:13–15; Colossians 2:16–17). Peter's behavior was dangerous to the budding Christian outreach. While as an apostle he was not explicitly teaching false doctrine with his words, nevertheless he implicitly sent a misleading message and gave a bad example by his action.

In the Gospel lesson, Luke 7:36–50, Jesus exposed the pretenses and wrong priorities of a Pharisee named Simon. It is crucial in understanding this text to note that when Jesus drew a contrast between Simon and the notoriously sinful woman who was washing and kissing His feet, He was not saying that the woman had done more fitting work to earn His forgiveness. Rather, He was contrasting their responses to forgiveness already offered, as in the story He had told in verses 41–42. Thus, when He said the woman was forgiven much for she had loved much (v. 47), the word *for* expressed evidence, not cause.

1. Who was acting self-righteously in each lesson? Do the actions of any of these people surprise you? Why?
   a. 2 Samuel 11:26–12:10, 13–15

   b. Galatians 2:11–21

   c. Luke 7:36–50

2. How did these people show that they did not want to be subject to the same standards they applied to others?
   a. 2 Samuel 11:26–12:10, 13–15 (see vv. 5–6)

   b. Galatians 2:11–21 (see vv. 12–13)

   c. Luke 7:36–50 (see v. 39)

3. How, specifically, was self-righteousness exposed in each lesson?
   a. 2 Samuel 11:26–12:10, 13–15 (see vv. 1–4, 7–10)

   b. Galatians 2:11–21 (see vv. 11, 14–16a)

   c. Luke 7:36–50 (see vv. 41–47)

4. Locate and restate God's Good News of forgiveness as it appears in each lesson.
   a. 2 Samuel 11:26–12:10, 13–15

b. Galatians 2:11–21

c. Luke 7:36–50

Connect

1. Through the life, death, and resurrection of Jesus Christ, God has furnished us with more forgiveness than our sins can ever deplete. In each lesson, the Good News eliminates any need for self-obtained human righteousness. What manifestations of self-righteousness could the people in our texts relinquish in faith?
   a. 2 Samuel 11:26–12:10, 13–15

   b. Galatians 2:11–21

   c. Luke 7:36–50

2. With a partner, take five minutes to brainstorm particular ways in which the Good News eliminates the need to demonstrate self-righteousness in your life. For example, you do not have to crave approval from others since the Lord has given you His great approval in Christ. Have the small groups report their best insights to the large group.

Vision

During This Week

1. Seek private absolution from your pastor.
2. Have a family devotion which features confession and a declaration of God's grace among family members.
3. Meditate on your Baptism as the great leveler—a daily drowning of the Old Adam but also bringing forth the new life in Christ.

Closing Worship

Sing stanza 6 of "Salvation unto Us Has Come" (*LW* 355).

>All blessing, honor, thanks and praise
>To Father, Son, and Spirit,
>The God who saved us by His grace;
>All glory to His merit
>O Triune God in heav'n above,
>You have revealed Your saving love;
>Your blessed name we hallow.

Scripture Lessons for Next Sunday

Read in preparation for the Fifth Sunday after Pentecost Zechariah 12:7–10; Galatians 3:23–29; and Luke 9:18–24.

Session 5

The Fifth Sunday after Pentecost

Zechariah 12:7–10; Galatians 3:23–29; Luke 9:18–24

Focus

Theme: *The Moment of Truth*

Law/Gospel Focus

We sometimes play games with God's law so we will forget its sharp accusation. When Jesus went to the cross as the Anointed One, the Christ of God, He exposed all our excuses even as He took away our sin. We now live victoriously, having been joined to Him through Baptism in His death and resurrection.

Objectives

That by the power of the Holy Spirit working through God's Word we might

1. see God's Law realistically as it closes off our self-saving delusions;
2. thank God, who baptized us into Christ's death and resurrection;
3. take up our crosses and follow Jesus.

Opening Worship

Sing or pray together stanzas 1–4 of "'Come Follow Me,' Said Christ the Lord" (*LW* 379).

"Come follow Me," said Christ, the Lord,
"All in My way abiding;
Your selfishness throw overboard,
Obey My call and guiding.
Oh, bear your crosses, and confide
In My example as your guide.

"I am the Light; I light the way,
A godly life displaying;
I help you walk as in the day;
I keep your feet from straying.
I am the Way, and well I show
How you should journey here below.

"My heart is rich in lowliness;
My soul with love is glowing;
My lips the words of grace express,
Their tones all gently flowing.
My heart, my mind, my strength, my all
To God I yield; on Him I call.

"I teach you how to shun and flee
What harms your soul's salvation;
Your heart from ev'ry guile to free,
From sin and its temptation.
I am the refuge of the soul
And lead you to your heav'nly goal."

Introduction

Think of someone you know who always seems to go above and beyond what is expected or required. Describe this person to the group.

The Gospel lesson shows us Jesus at a turning point in His work. He has done so much, but now He tells the disciples that, on top of everything, He must die. How do you think they felt? How do you feel about what Jesus said next—that anyone who follows Him must take up the cross?

Inform

Select group members to play the two characters in the following three-part skit. After each part is read aloud, answer the accompanying questions.

Reader 1 (*on telephone*): Yes, operator, this is Mr. Kinniscope, producer of the TV show "To Tell the Truth." You have a call from our man in Galilee? Fine.

Reader 2: Hello, Mr. Kinniscope? Jimmy Eager here. I hope you'll agree that I've got someone who will be the greatest contestant in game-show history.

Reader 1: Why don't you tell me a bit about this contestant?

Reader 2: His name is Jesus. He's a traveling preacher who has a group of disciples.

Reader 1: Hold on. If this guy is a preacher, He doesn't stick out like a sore thumb, does He? On our show the panel is supposed to guess the contestant's identity. We don't want to make it too easy.

Reader 2: No problem. Simply to look at Him, Jesus seems just like everyone else.

Reader 1: But we don't want the opposite problem, either. He isn't boring, is He?

Reader 2: Definitely not. He… has unique qualities.

Reader 1: I'm getting the uncomfortable feeling that you haven't told me everything.

Reader 2: Sir, you can read me like a book. I've been saving the best 'til last: He's the Christ of God. (*Pause.*) Now, I know what you're going to say: It seems too good to be true that the ancient prophecies are finally coming to pass!

Reader 1: Are you sure you're feeling all right?

Reader 2: Sir, I know that many people have given up on the old promises …

Reader 1: Let's just say we've moved on. We've seen the culture of Greece, the power of Rome, status in the world—things like that. Besides, the old religion was full of laws and the sternest accusations for anyone who didn't toe the line. It was stifling. Who needed that? Remember, Eager, we have to put on programs for an audience that is influenced by the times.

Reader 2: They may be influenced by the times, but …

Reader 1: Religion itself is influenced by the times. It's no secret that these days we don't pay too much attention to the Law—not if we want to keep our sanity. We don't appoint high priests the way the Bible says. We follow the world's models of power. Everybody does. Why do you suppose your friend Jesus comes along claiming to be the Messiah, and people yawn?

Reader 2: But they aren't just yawning. They're talking. The disciples told Jesus how some say He's Elijah, or some other old prophet, or John the Baptist.

Reader 1: Who's that last one?

Reader 2: He was a preacher who said Jesus is the Christ. Herod had him killed.

Reader 1: So there's danger in saying that Jesus is the Christ. Maybe that's why more people don't say it.

1. While Mr. Kinniscope is right about God's law in a way, he is mostly wrong. Evaluate what he says in light of Galatians 3:23–25.

2. Is it good that Jesus seemed like everyone else? Why or why not?

3. How is it dangerous today to say that Jesus is the Christ?

Reader 2: Sir, what do you think about having Jesus on the show?

Reader 1: It's clear that he's a hot property. If He has a big following, it could boost ratings. All right; why not? The panel will face a real challenge from Jesus if no one can make sense out of who He is or what He's doing.

Reader 2: That's not quite true, sir. I know who He is: He's the Christ of God.

Reader 1: Okay. If you really buy this stuff, can you tell me what Jesus is up to?

Reader 2: Jesus told His disciples, "The Son of Man must suffer many things and be rejected by the elders, chief priests and teachers of the law, and He must be killed, and on the third day be raised to life."

Reader 1: I can see why people are confused; I'm kind of fuzzy myself. You're saying that this Jesus is the Christ, the Messiah. You say He does things only God can do. But then you tell me that He will be rejected and die! Doesn't it seem strange that this is what the Messiah is going to do?

Reader 2: Maybe it's what being the Messiah is all about.

Reader 1: Oh, come on.

Reader 2: I'm serious. Why else would Jesus make such a big point about His suffering just after the disciples confessed that He is the Christ? He wanted to connect the cross to His very identity as the Messiah, as the Christ. Didn't God say through the prophet, "They will look on Me, the one they have pierced"?

Reader 1: You're saying that the way of the Christ means death.

Reader 2: It means commitment: complete, overriding commitment to people—people who neither know nor care about Him, people who find it impossible to live under God's demands and who have forgotten His promises.

Reader 1: Pardon my cynical streak, but why should He do all that?

Reader 2: Because He's faithful. He loves people. He loves us. And we need Him.

Reader 1: For what? To take us back to days we've outgrown?

Reader 2: No. We need Him to answer a need we never outgrow, our need for God's forgiveness. The law of God closes off our every hope for self-salvation. We can't be saved by ourselves; we can only be saved by Him. Believing in Him means that I receive from God something I could never come up with on my own. It means that I am with Him in His death.

Reader 1: With Him in His death?

Reader 2: It starts with Him being for me as the Suffering Servant of prophecy, my substitute before God. God delights in me because of Him. I am now God's son because Jesus, God's eternal Son, is also my Brother. But that's not all He says. He adds, "If anyone would come after Me, he must deny himself and take up his cross daily and follow Me." It's like having a moment of truth every day: not only telling the truth, but His truth having its way in me, expressed through me to others as I go from death to resurrection with Him.

4. It is an opinion of some Jews, now as well as in the first century, that the Messiah would not come until the end of the world. Respond to this idea based on the words, "They will look on Me, the one they have pierced."

5. "The way of the Christ means death." Why is this such a hard saying?

6. How do we join Jesus in His death and resurrection? See Galatians 3:27.

Connect

Reader 1: Speaking of telling the truth, we still have a show to discuss.

Reader 2: Do you want Jesus?

Reader 1: Let's say I don't believe in Him as you do, but He'd be a great contestant.

Reader 2: Could we let the audience do the guessing when He appears on the program?

Reader 1: Not the panel?

Reader 2: They could join in, but the audience has to confront Jesus sooner or later.

Reader 1: Not on our show, they don't.

Reader 2: Don't you see? It will heighten the drama! It'll be great.

Reader 1: It will scare people to death. We can't do that to our audience.

Reader 2: You want them to sit there, calm and detached, waiting for a few laughs?

Reader 1: That's what they do with every other guest.

Reader 2: He isn't every other guest! With Jesus, there has to be a moment of truth.

Reader 1: Eager, I admire your conviction, but I can't let you do this. If Jesus wants to confront people, let Him buy air time like everyone else.

Reader 2: He's out to buy more than that. He's buying back the whole world. That's what being the Christ is all about. Our audience should hear about Him.

Reader 1: You're playing with dynamite. Keep on like this and you'll lose your job.

Reader 2: "Whoever wants to save his life will lose it, but whoever loses his life for Me will save it." That's Jesus' approach, and it's good enough for me.

Reader 1: You want to go the way of the cross.

Reader 2: I want to go the way of the Christ.

Reader 1: When you play "To Tell the Truth," it's for high stakes.

Reader 2: It's no game. It's a way of life: the life God gives, and the life I live in Him.

1. How are today's Christians tempted to take the edge off the confrontation between Jesus and the unbelieving world?

2. When you have a moment of truth, how can you keep the spotlight on Christ and what He has done?

Vision

During This Week

Use your crosses as occasions to thank Christ for how He endured the cross.

Closing Worship

Sing or pray together stanza 5 of "'Come Follow Me,' Said Christ the Lord" (*LW* 379).

> Then let us follow Christ, our Lord
> And take the cross appointed
> And, firmly clinging to the word,
> In suff'ring be undaunted.
> For those who bear the battle's strain
> The crown of heav'nly life obtain.

Scripture Lessons for Next Sunday

In preparation for the Sixth Sunday after Pentecost, read 1 Kings 19:14–21; Galatians 5:1, 13–25; Luke 9:51–62.

Session 6

The Sixth Sunday after Pentecost

1 Kings 19:14–21; Galatians 5:1, 13–25; Luke 9:51–62

Focus

Theme: *Great Discipleship Comes from the Great Lord*

Law/Gospel Focus

Christian discipleship always comes by association—association with Christ. Discipleship is a great calling, not because of its breathtaking activity, but because the disciple of Christ has the greatest Master, who became a servant to win for us forgiveness of sins and eternal life by His death on the cross.

Objectives

That by the enabling power of the Holy Spirit working through God's Word we might
1. sharpen our Biblical understanding of the nature of Christian discipleship;
2. look to Jesus as the unique one on whom our discipleship depends;
3. rely on Him to provide us forgiveness, strength, and salvation;
4. bear the fruit of His Spirit.

Opening Worship

Pray the prayer "For the Holy Spirit" (*LW*, p. 124)

Almighty and everlasting God, of Your great mercy in Jesus Christ You have granted us forgiveness of sin and all things pertaining to life and godliness. Therefore send us Your Holy Spirit that He may so rule our hearts that we, being ever mindful of

Introduction

What do you think of when you hear the word *disciple?* You may
wish to consult a standard dictionary or try to formulate quickly a biblical definition, based on your knowledge of the New Testament.

What makes a disciple a disciple? Does being a "disciple" differ
from being a "Christian"?

Inform

Concentrate first on Luke 9:51–62. Jesus, having the determination ("set His face") to go to Jerusalem (v. 51), refuses to call down the
fire of divine judgment on a group of Samaritan detractors and then
talks with three would-be followers on the road.

It might be tempting, at first glance, to think of this text basically
as a list of disciple dos and don'ts: *don't* be like hotheaded James and
John; *do* be dedicated, as Jesus told the three on the road. But the
passage itself puts the emphasis not on the disciple's identity, but
rather on Jesus' identity. In particular, this section of Luke contrasts
Jesus with the Old Testament prophet Elijah.

1. How did …
    Elijah respond to the Samaritans (2 Kings 1:9–12)?

Jesus respond to the Samaritans (Luke 9:52–55)?

2. What did Elijah prove in his response (2 Kings 1:10)?

   What did Jesus prove in His response (Luke 9:34–35)?

3. How urgent was it for ...
   Elisha to respond to Elijah (1 Kings 19:19–21)?

   the Samaritan to respond to Jesus (Luke 9:59–62)?

4. What was God's plan for ...
   Elijah (2 Kings 2:11)?

   Jesus (Luke 9:51 and also 9:30–31)?

The demands entailed by discipleship mount high, *but*

- this point comes as no surprise when we recall just whose disciples we are.
- our Teacher is the one who went to a shameful death in Jerusalem for us and for all.
- great discipleship is continual walking with the great Lord.

Connect

We have noted the pivotal position which Jesus alone has in the life of the disciple. Our Lord gives us His own brand of compassion and determination.

But the life of the disciple is not all rosebuds without thorns. In this section we will look at two challenging circumstances that often confront disciples of Christ.

1. What happens when the Teacher seems so far away and you, His student (disciple), find yourself disappointed—needing help, but not seeming to get any? Based on 1 Kings 19, we might call this phenomenon the "Elijah syndrome." It results when we lose track of how *great* discipleship comes from a *great* Lord.

   In the first part of 1 Kings 19, Elijah met with sudden, total reversal. Shortly before he had won—by God's power—a showdown with the prophets of Baal. But the tables had turned, and he was taking it *very* hard. As much as Elijah had once been filled with zeal, he now found himself bone-tired, burned out, disillusioned. Wicked queen Jezebel threatened his very life. He ran away. Out of Israel he ran, all the way down to the Sinai Peninsula. He figured that he must have been the last prophet of the Lord left, but he didn't want to be a prophet anymore. If someone was out to kill him, that was just as well. Elijah wanted to die.

   Here are some questions that may have occurred to Elijah. Perhaps they sound familiar.

   - How did I go through so much effort, but have so little to show for it?
   - Where did I fail?
   - How am I going to put the pieces back together now, after all this?
   - Why should I even try anymore?

Now notice what the Lord did for Elijah:

a. He came to Elijah and spoke to him—not in wind, earthquake, and fire, but in a still, small voice (1 Kings 19:11–13). What was the Lord telling Elijah in this act? How can God's action help us today?

b. He assured Elijah, as the prophet went about his work, that there were 7,000 God-fearing people left who had not bowed the knee to the false god Baal (1 Kings 19:18). What was the Lord telling Elijah in these words? How can these words help us today?

2. What happens when you're not feeling quite as low as Elijah was, but you sense that your discipleship is dragging? Remember, great discipleship comes from being in the presence of the great Lord.

Galatians 5:1, 13–25 is a good text to keep in mind. We will apply it to our lives by way of a little story. Follow along as a volunteer reads it.

This is about a young man, Polycarp, who is a fruit bearer. Actually, ever since graduation he has driven a fruit truck for his dad.

While he was in high school, Polycarp longed to be free of controls at home. But it wasn't until he became a fruit bearer that he realized how hard self-control could be. One night at a truck stop, his thoughts were consumed with wooing pretty girls, playing a cruel practical joke on a rival driver, or going out and getting drunk. But he ended up not doing any of those things, because he wanted to be a good fruit-bearer. He decided to go to bed.

Since he was a Christian, Polycarp used to read his Bible before going to sleep. That night he hit upon the passage about the desires of the flesh which oppose the desires of the Spirit (Galatians 5:13–25). No wonder he had such a problem with evil thoughts earlier! That was part of the battle! The Bible said that those who make a practice of such things will not inherit the kingdom of God (Galatians 5:21), and that scared him. Further down the page, though, Polycarp ran across God's answer to the problem: He kills us. "Those who belong to Christ Jesus have crucified the flesh with its passions and desires" (Galatians 5:24). Polycarp thought of how he had been linked with the Lord through Baptism. When Christ died, Polycarp died, for Christ took the sin of all. Now no sin, no guilt or accusation could touch Polycarp. Now he was alive in the risen Christ!

Polycarp awakened the next day, eager to get on the road and bear fruit. He went to the cafe for breakfast. He found the waitress rude and the service slow, but he kept telling himself, "patience, kindness." After eating, he found his rig blocked in by another truck. He was shouting in exasperation, "gentleness, self-control," until the other driver came and he got under way.

A bit later he found the fruit in the back of the truck going bad because he had forgotten to set the temperature control. Now what could he do? Go to a lab and say, "Make me some fruit?" No!!! You don't *make* fruit. It *grows*.

Polycarp started reading again: "If you are led by the Spirit, you are not under law" (Galatians 5:18). Then it hit him. You can't force the fruit of the Spirit. He had tried to do so at the truck stop. But he could not get himself to be joyful, peaceful, etc. simply by telling himself to be joyful.

People do not make fruit. It grows. So with the fruit of the Spirit: the Holy Spirit creates it. Polycarp's job was to bear it.

The Spirit creates out of nothing. Polycarp knew that he himself was a sinner, a slave to the flesh. Only the Holy Spirit could cultivate the qualities of Jesus in Polycarp's life, and He did it by removing Polycarp's sin as far as east from west. Since Polycarp was connected to Christ, God's creative power was in his life. "I am the Vine, you are the branches," said Jesus. A good tree produces good fruit.

Polycarp finally got a new load of fruit. But soon he came upon a highway roadblock, and the fruit inspector. Judgment time for his fruit! The inspector looked around and told Polycarp, "I work for your dad. Go on through." When Polycarp asked about imperfections in the fruit, the inspector said, "as far as your dad is concerned, *you're* hauling the fruit, so it's okay."

Here the story of Polycarp the trucker breaks down. Our fruit inspectors wouldn't say such a thing. But God's grace defies all comparison. Not only does He accept us; He also accepts our fruit, miserable as it is. He is the fruit inspector, and in Christ He is perfectly satisfied with us and our fruit.

We are not (1) automatic fruit-hauling machines; (2) fruit creators; (3) fruit inspectors. We disciples are fruit bearers!

Have you ever felt like an automatic fruit hauler, a fruit creator, or a fruit inspector? What blocks fruit bearing in the Christian life? How does it help you to know that Christian disciples are fruit bearers?

Vision

During This Week

1. Be sensitive to someone you know who is battling the "Elijah syndrome." Lend that person the encouragement of Christ's presence in the Word.
2. Meditate on your Baptism as a power pack for Christian living. See Romans 6:1–14.

Closing Worship

Sing or pray together "You Will I Love, My Strength" (*LW* 375).

> You will I love, my strength, my tower;
> You will I love, my hope, my joy;
> You will I love with all my power,
> With fervor time cannot destroy.
> You will I love, O Light divine,
> So long as life is mine.
>
> You will I love, my life, my Savior,
> You are my best, my truest friend;
> You will I love and praise forever,
> For never shall Your kindness end.
> Your love for me casts out my fear,
> You are my Savior dear.

I thank You, Jesus, sun from heaven,
Whose radiance has brought light to me;
I thank You, who has richly forgiven
All that could make me glad and free.
I thank You that my soul is healed
With love that You revealed.

Oh, keep me watchful, then, and humble,
And never suffer me to stray;
Uphold me when my feet would stumble,
And keep me faithful to Your way.
Fill all my nature with Your light,
O Radiance strong and bright!

You will I love, my crown of gladness;
You will I love, my God and Lord,
Within the darkest depths of sadness,
And not for hope of high reward—
For Your own sake, O Light divine,
So long as life is mine!

Scripture Lessons for Next Sunday

Read in preparation for the Seventh Sunday after Pentecost Isaiah
66:10–14; Galatians 6:1–10, 14–16; and Luke 10:1–12, 16, [17–20].

Session 7

The Seventh Sunday after Pentecost

Isaiah 66:10–14; Galatians 6:1–10, 14–16;
Luke 10:1–12, 16, [17–20]

Focus

Theme: *Half the Sorrow, Double the Joy*

Law/Gospel Focus

Enclosed within our sin, we want to go it alone in life and spurn all help from God and man. But the life-bestowing Lord, who carried our self-centered guilt to His cross has left it there. He comforts and upholds us through His powerful Gospel and His body the church as a center for love and forgiveness.

Objectives

That by the enabling power of the Holy Spirit working through God's Word we might

1. acknowledge our need for the help God gives through His Word and the community of Christians;
2. receive from Him the comfort brought by His Word and the people who share it;
3. bear the burdens of others.

Opening Worship

Pray together the prayer "For the Afflicted and Distressed," (*LW*, p. 126).

Almighty and everlasting God, the consolation of the sorrowful and the strength of the weak, may the prayers of those who in any tribulation or distress cry to You graciously come before You, so that in all their necessities they may mark and receive Your manifold help and comfort; through Jesus Christ, our Lord. Amen.

Introduction

Can you tell a story based on your own experience that resembles any of these situations?

- Lost on a car trip, and despite his wife's urging, the man at the wheel does not want to stop and ask for directions.
- Children who cannot perform a difficult task will often not rest until you give them a chance to give it a try. "*I* want to do it," they will say if you offer to help.
- You experience great frustration at work when you have to learn a new computer program, and you find it deeply embarrassing if a co-worker notices you struggling with the training manual.

Why are we often so stubborn? Why do we want to solve our problems all on our own without asking for help? What does it take finally to get us to break down and ask questions? How do you feel when you do get the help you need: relief, failure, something else?

An old proverb says shared sorrow is half the sorrow; shared joy is double the joy. In the Scripture passages for today, we have our Lord's invitation to cut our sorrow and double our joy in fellowship with Him and with His people.

═══════════ Inform ═══════════

Isaiah 66:10–14, a text from the last chapter of this great prophetic book, looks ahead to how the Lord would give His comfort both to and through His church ("Jerusalem").

Galatians 6:1–10, 14–16 constitutes most of Paul's closing charge and comfort to the Galatians, who had been lead astray by the legalism of the Judaizers. Not in order for them to attain salvation, but rather due to the salvation already theirs in Christ, Paul reminds them of their responsibilities to one another. They are fellow members of Christ's body because Jesus bore the burden of sin on the cross. *Note:* There is no conflict between verses 2 and 5. The word translated "burdens" in the NIV in verse 2 means a crushing weight. But the word translated "load" in the NIV in verse 5 denotes a load which an animal could bear or a cargo which a ship could carry—a manageable load.)

Luke 10:1–12, 16 [17–20] tells of how Jesus sent out 72 "advance men" to herald His final preaching tour on His way to Jerusalem and His ultimate death and resurrection there. He instructs them about the work they are to do; then He tells them of the dignity they have as they carry His Word. Finally, He rejoices with them over their successes but more so over their salvation. Answer the following questions.

1. In each lesson, what is the particular need (expressed or implied) for God's help or comfort?
    a. Isaiah 66:10–14

    b. Luke 10:1–12, 16 [17–20]

    c. Galatians 6:1–10, 14–16

2. In each text, what specific comfort or help does God give?
    a. Isaiah 66:10–14

    b. Luke 10:1–12, 16 (17–20)

    c. Galatians 6:1–10, 14–16

Connect

1. Take a few minutes to think about what burden(s) prove difficult or impossible for you at times to bear. Pray silently that the Lord, who knows your need before you even ask, would give you His power to bear this burden in His name. But do not stop there. Ask yourself: How can fellow members of the body of Christ help you? Are you afraid to ask for help? Why?

2. Brainstorm a list of things which you think members of your congregation can do to ease the burdens of one another. Add specifically what you as an individual can do.

As you listen to what others say, you might find someone else in the group who can help you bear a burden, or whose burden you can help to bear.

Vision

During This Week

1. Remind yourself through Scripture reading, hymns, and devotions etc. that your name is written in the book of life.
2. If you have a pressing burden, don't delay. Ask a brother or sister in Christ to help you with it. At very least, talk to your pastor or some other Christian about why you are reluctant to ask for help.
3. If someone asks you for help in bearing a burden, take the advice of Paul: do not become weary of doing good.

Closing Worship

Sing or pray together "Blest Be the Tie That Binds," (*LW* 295).

> Blest be the tie that binds
> Our hearts in Christian love;
> The unity of heart and mind
> Is like to that above.
>
> Before our Father's throne
> We pour our ardent prayers;
> Our fears, our hopes, our aims are one,
> Our comforts and our cares.
>
> We share our mutual woes,
> Our mutual burdens bear,
> And often for each other flows
> The sympathizing tear.
>
> From sorrow, toil, and pain
> And sin we shall be free,
> And perfect love and friendship reign
> Through all eternity.

Scripture Lessons for Next Sunday

Read in preparation for the Eighth Sunday after Pentecost Deuteronomy 30:9–14; Colossians 1:1–14; and Luke 10:25–27.

Session 8

The Eighth Sunday after Pentecost

Deuteronomy 30:9–14; Colossians 1:1–14; Luke 10:25–27

Focus

Theme: *What Do I Do? Nothing and Everything!*

Law/Gospel Focus

God shows that every attempt to justify ourselves is a dead end. Instead, He Himself has qualified us, rescued us, and forgiven us, through Christ's work accomplished outside of ourselves. We respond in joyfulness and thanksgiving to the Savior who loved us and gave Himself for us!

Objectives

That by the enabling power of the Holy Spirit working through God's Word we might
1. forsake all the excuses which we so readily make;
2. "thank the Father, who made us fit to share the inheritance of the saints in the light" (Colossians 1:12);
3. aim "to please Him in every way" (Colossians 1:10).

Opening Worship

Sing or pray together "Seek Where You May" (*LW* 358).
> Seek where you may
> To find a way,
> Restless, toward your salvation.
> My heart is stilled,
> On Christ I build,
> He is the one foundation.
> His Word is sure,
> His works endure;
> He overthrows
> All evil foes;
> Through Him I more than conquer.

Seek whom you may
To be your stay,
None can redeem his brother.
All helpers failed;
This man prevailed,
The God-man and none other
Our Servant-King
Of whom we sing.
We're justified
Because He died,
The guilty being guiltless.

Seek Him alone,
Do not postpone;
Let Him your soul deliver.
All you who thirst,
Go to Him first
Whose grace flows like a river.
Seek Him indeed
In ev'ry need;
He will impart
To ev'ry heart
The fullness of His treasure.

My heart's delight,
My crown most bright,
O Christ, my joy forever.
Not wealth nor pride
Nor fortune's tide
Our bonds of love shall sever.
You are my Lord;
Your precious Word
Shall guide my way
And help me stay
Forever in Your presence.

Introduction

Two or three church members occasionally said to their pastor, "I think you should get tougher on sin in your sermons." Rather predictably, the pastor noticed, there followed a suggestion that he preach more on the subjects of drunkenness and/or swearing. He also noticed that the people who were making the suggestions did not have a noticeable problem with the use of foul language, and they did not drink. Why do you suppose they wanted their pastor to preach more about these subjects? If you stood in the pastor's shoes, what might you say to the church members?

Inform

In Deuteronomy 30:9–14 God, through Moses, told the Israelites that He had given them His commands in clear and plain words. Still more, He hinted that by His Word of promise, the Gospel, He would enable them to love these commands in addition merely to knowing them.

In Colossians 1:1–14, Paul told the Colossian Christians how he and his colleagues prayed for them. He thanked God for their faith, love, and hope. Paul also asked God to continue their growth in wisdom and works, since He has saved them in Christ.

In Luke 10:25–37, Jesus conversed with an expert in the Law who wanted to "justify himself" (v. 29) in the face of the Law's all-encompassing demands. Jesus did not play the man's game of trying to make "neighbor" an abstract and correspondingly vague concept; in the story of the Good Samaritan, He talked about *active* love toward a particular person. In so doing, Jesus described God's idea of love.

To explore these texts further, play a game like "Jeopardy." For each reference the answer will be given to you; in every case, that answer will be either "everything" or "nothing." Your challenge, as usual in "Jeopardy," will be to formulate a *question* to which either "everything" or "nothing" is the correct answer. Be sure to base your question on the Bible passage under consideration. (On the "game board" below, the first question is filled in as an example. You provide the rest.)

VERSE	ANSWER	QUESTION
Deuteronomy 30:10	Everything	In what did God want the Israelites to obey Him?
Deuteronomy 30:11–13	Nothing	
Deuteronomy 30:14	Nothing	
Luke 10:25–28	Everything	

Luke 10:29	Nothing
Luke 10:30–37	Everything
Colossians 1:12	Nothing
Colossians 1:13	Everything
Colossians 1:14	Everything
Colossians 1:5–6	Everything
Colossians 1:10	Everything

In the Old Testament lesson, God said He demands that people do *everything* that the Law requires. But, like the Israelites of old, we can do *nothing* to keep the Law with our hands unless we first love it in our heart.

The Gospel lesson showed us a man who, despite his expertise, did not love the Law. The goal of Jesus, in His dialog with the man, was to bring him face-to-face with the fact that ultimately he could do *nothing* to keep God's Law as God required.

This line of thought, as we have traced it so far, does not prove to be very encouraging. It speaks to us God's condemning Law, underscoring that God demands *everything* but we can give Him *nothing*.

The unmerited gift of salvation comes only from Christ. In Him alone do we have forgiveness of our sins, since He paid the ransom-price to set us free (Colossians 1:14). In Christ, God has done *everything* to qualify us to receive the inheritance of the saints (v. 12) and to rescue us from darkness and transplant us into the Kingdom of His beloved Son (v. 13). There remains *nothing* we can do to save ourselves. By going to Jerusalem to die, innocently yet by the will of God, Jesus Himself gave to sinners the very same sort of complete, caring, self-sacrificing love which He was demanding of the expert of the Law.

This remarkable Savior kindles a response in us. While we can do *nothing* to inherit eternal life, nonetheless now, by His power, we do and suffer *everything* in our desire to please Him (Colossians

1:10–11). Receiving from His abundance, we have come not only to know God's law, but to love it. For the Gospel that is proclaimed with the mouth has gone into our hearts (Deuteronomy 30:14) to forgive, reassure, and regenerate; thus, it produces fruit (Colossians 1:5–6, 10).

Connect

1. Discuss the following quote from Luther's treatise on "The Freedom of a Christian." What does it have to do with our discussion? With your life?

   "A Christian is a perfectly free lord of all, subject to none. A Christian is a perfectly dutiful servant of all, subject to all" (*Luther's Works* 31:344).
2. How does the Gospel enable you to love the Law?

Vision

During This Week

1. Celebrate your freedom in the Gospel. When you are tempted to make up excuses, or to hold yourself up to a flattering comparison with someone else, remember and rejoice over the riches you have in Christ alone!
2. Read Luther's treatise on "The Freedom of a Christian."
3. Recall that God does not delight in our self-chosen works. Certain that Jesus Christ has covered your sins, determine what aspects of your God-given role in life (vocation) you are neglecting in favor of things you do not really have to do.

Closing Worship

Pray the prayer "For Likeness to Christ" (*LW*, p. 125):

O God, by the patient suffering of Your only-begotten Son You have beaten down the pride of the old enemy. Now help us, we humbly pray, rightly to treasure in our hearts all that our Lord has of His goodness borne for our sake that after His example we may bear with patience all that is adverse to us; through Jesus Christ, our Lord. Amen.

Scripture Lessons for Next Sunday

Read in preparation for the Ninth Sunday after Pentecost Genesis 18:1–10; Colossians 1:21–28; and Luke 10:38–42.

Session 9

The Ninth Sunday after Pentecost

Genesis 18:1–14; Colossians 1:21–28; Luke 10:38–42

Focus

Theme: *To Love Is to Listen*

Law/Gospel Focus

We are to devote ourselves to hearing the Word of God attentively so He can teach us. In the presence of Christ we acknowledge that His gifts of forgiveness of sins and eternal life are more valuable than anything we can ever give Him.

Objectives

Through the enabling power of the Holy Spirit working through the Word of God we will

1. learn the value of slowing down our activity so that we have the opportunity to experience the joy of listening to what God has done for us in Christ;
2. rejoice in our status as sin-cleansed saints through Christ's completed work of reconciliation;
3. remember that "everything in the Christian church is so ordered that we may daily obtain full forgiveness of sins through the Word" (*Large Catechism* II 55).

Opening Worship

Pray Together:
Leader: Slow me down, Lord,
Participants: Steady my hurried steps.
Leader: Remind me each day that there is more to life
Participants: Than increasing its speed.
Leader: Slow me down, Lord,

Participants: Speak and quiet my anxious spirit.

(By kind permission of Dominican Publications. 42 Parnell Sq., Dublin 1, Ireland.)

Introduction

Listening—genuine, patient listening—is important. The great 17th-century English scientist Isaac Newton once remarked that if he had made any improvement in the sciences, it was owing more to "patient attention" than to anything else. A contemporary communications guru, John Gray, author of the best-selling 1992 book *Men Are from Mars, Women Are from Venus* says that one of the major causes of divorce is that women come home from work every day wanting to talk and their partners don't know how to listen.

The great reformer Luther once described the church as the *Mundhaus* (God's "speech-house"). He said that the proper organ of the Christian is the ear, because it receives God's speech. Often Jesus said, "He who has ears, let him hear." His words indicate that we have been given ears for listening.

Listening is a God-given ability. But like other such abilities, it needs to be cultivated.

1. List two things that you think must happen for an individual to be able to be a good listener. See James 1:19a; and Luke 10:40 with Matthew 13:22.

2. Describe one or two techniques you have used to set up a situation for getting someone's undivided attention, or for you to be able to give your undivided attention to another.

3. When we give up some precious time in our busy schedules to let another person share thoughts or hurts with us, what are we indicating to that person about how we view him or her?

Inform

Review the following summaries of the Scripture lessons for the Ninth Sunday after Pentecost.

Genesis 18:1–14—While still at Mamre near Hebron, Abraham invites three strangers to be his guests. He and Sarah prepare a feast for the strangers. One of the guests is God Himself, who temporarily has assumed visible form. He promises that aged Sarah will have a child in a year. She laughs to herself when she overhears the promise. God repeats His promise.

Colossians 1:21–28—Having described Christ's preeminence over all creation, Paul exhorts Christians not to be moved from the hope presented in the Gospel. He proclaimed to them the "mystery," that is, Christ's ministry, that resulted in their perfection and hope of glory.

Luke 10:38–42—Facing growing hostility from religious enemies, Jesus is welcomed into the home of Martha and her sister Mary. While Martha bustled about preparing a meal for Jesus, Mary sits like a student at Jesus' feet, listening to Him. She receives Jesus' commendation for being occupied with listening *to* Him rather than being occupied with things *for* Him, like Martha.

All three lessons contain an exhortation to proper hearing of God's Word. Based on the lessons, discuss the following questions.

1. What similarities can you identify between the Old Testament and the Gospel lesson?

2. Why was it natural for Sarah to laugh? Does God disqualify her from receiving His special gift to this family because of her actions? What does He do in response? What comfort is there for us in His response?

3. What is the significance of the name given to the child who was born of God's promise? See Genesis 21:3.

4. In the Epistle lesson Paul provides a before and after description of people. Why would unbelievers laugh at such a description of members of your congregation?

5. In a world still ravaged by ethnic wars, where families and individuals are alienated from each other as well as from God, what is the wondrous "mystery" that Christians have been given to reveal to others? See Matthew 13:11; Ephesians 3:12, 6:19.

6. Jesus continues to identify Himself closely with those who suffer because they are His followers. See Acts 9:1–5. What astonishing statement can Paul therefore make? See Colossians 1:24.

7. Consider this situation: A special guest was coming to my home. I decided he was worth the "red carpet treatment." So the house was thoroughly cleaned, the dining table had my best dinnerware upon it, and I even purchased a special floral centerpiece. When he came I lavished great service on him. He, for his part, was most gracious. When he left I felt really good about all I had done, and yet something was bothering me. For a while I couldn't figure it out. Then a question arose within me: What did he really want from me? Suddenly there came other questions. Why had he come? What did he want to give me? Whatever it was, I gave him no opportunity to extend it to me.

   This situation is similar to what the Gospel lesson describes in the home of Martha and Mary. See Matthew 13:22; Luke 9:35;

Colossians 2:2–3; and Proverbs 8:34–35 to help you understand what happened that day in their home.

═══ **Connect** ═══

1. Your Bible class leader will read you a well-known section of Scripture. After the reading he will ask a series of questions. Indicate your answer by checking either the YES or NO column.

   YES   NO

   a.

   b.

   c.

   d.

2. In what sense would you say that this statement is true: "Those who cannot listen, cannot learn"? Think, for example, about a parent's training of a young child. Why is it especially important that we take hearing the Word of God seriously? See Acts 11:14; 1 Corinthians 1:21; 1 Thessalonians 1:4–5; Romans 10:17.

3. In his letter to the Colossians, Paul exhorts them not to move away from the hope held before them in the Gospel. What are some of the things—either in your own life or the lives of others— that could move you "from the hope held out in the gospel?"

4. Can you describe one of God's blessings that caused you to laugh afterwards when you remembered how unsolvable you once thought a problem was?

5. The answers to the following questions do not need to be shared. Listen to each statement, take it to heart, then check either the *yes* or *no* column.

YES	NO	
❑	❑	My priorities are God—first, family—second, work—third.
❑	❑	I don't laugh enough with the Lord over problems.
❑	❑	I am more like Martha than like Mary.

Vision

During This Week

1. Take a friend or family member out to lunch. Be attentive to the feelings behind the words spoken. Be eager to empathize so that you can respond to what is said and not said.
2. Carve out time in your busy schedule to read a small portion of Scripture. Before you begin reading, pray, "Speak, Lord, Your servant is listening."
3. When you are in church (possibly, just before the sermon), pray this prayer: "Lord, what are You saying to me this day?"

Closing Worship

Sing or pray together stanza 5 of "One Thing's Needful" (*LW* 277).

Wisdom's highest, noblest treasure,
Jesus, is revealed in you.
Let me find in You my pleasure,
Make my will and actions true,
Humility there and simplicity reigning,
In paths of true wisdom my steps ever training.
If I learn from Jesus this knowledge divine,
The blessing of heavenly wisdom is mine.

Scripture Lessons for Next Sunday

Read Genesis 18:20–32; Colossians 2:6–15; and Luke 11:1–13 in preparation for the Tenth Sunday after Pentecost.

Session 10

The Tenth Sunday
after Pentecost

Genesis 18:20–32; Colossians 2:6–15; Luke 11:1–13

Focus

Theme: *The Confidence to Ask Persistently*

Law/Gospel Focus

Often our prayers are either too self-centered or we lack the confidence that God is willing to grant the request. Through His crucifixion Christ has removed all obstacles to God. He has revealed the heavenly Father, who is more than willing to give to His children all they need.

Objectives

By the enabling power of the Holy Spirit working through God's Word we will

1. remain confident in God's love and wisdom so that we persist in prayer;
2. broaden the content of our petitions to include not only our own spiritual needs and those of our loved ones but also the spiritual needs of those who are presently our enemies;
3. become more spiritually disciplined in our daily life so that we devote greater time to private prayer.

Opening Worship

Pray together:

Leader: O God, our heavenly Father,
Participants: We thank You for the privilege of coming to You
             with all our needs and the needs of our world.
Leader: O God, our Lord Jesus Christ,

Introduction

Those who are in love constantly seek opportunities to talk *about*
their beloved. They also spend a lot of time talking *to* their beloved.
There is perhaps no better mark of closeness and affection between
two people than when free, heartfelt communication flows back and
forth between them. Similarly, the Christian life is not simply talking
about God; we also speak *to* our God.

1. If you were in complete control of all around you for just one hour,
   what would you do to make this world a safer place? Do you think
   the world would vote to extend your power beyond that hour?
   Why or why not?

2. In a classic 16th-century novel by John Bunyan, *Pilgrim's Progress*,
   there is a scene in which the chief character is led into a room to
   behold a man who had a rake in his hand and who could only look
   downward. Over the man's head hovered an angel offering him a
   golden crown in exchange for the rake. But the poor man continued raking the scraps on the floor, never once looking up, unaware
   of the glorious crown that was offered to him.

   Our present society has lost the sense of transcendence, as it
   bows to the philosophy of secular materialism and humanism.
   Human accomplishments and visible pleasures are often considered the only things of worth. How has this philosophy impover-
   ished the life of people around you?

3. When an individual prays and values the opportunity to speak to God, what is this person acknowledging about himself/herself and his/her life's goals?

Inform

Read the following summaries of the Scripture lessons for the Tenth Sunday after Pentecost.

Genesis 18:20–32—God tells Abraham that He has come to destroy the cities of Sodom and Gomorrah because their sins have grown intolerable. Six times Abraham intercedes for the cities, appealing to God's mercy and justice, so that any righteous among the people will not wrongly suffer.

Colossians 2:6–15—Paul encourages Christians to live their lives confident in Christ. Through Baptism they have become beneficiaries of the full blessings and victory which Christ gained for them at His cross.

Luke 11:1–13—After Jesus finished praying, one of His disciples asked Him to teach them to pray as John the Baptizer had taught his disciples to pray. Jesus responded to this request with a model for prayer, often known as "the Lord's Prayer." He then told a humorous parable about a neighbor who was persistent in an attempt to borrow bread. Jesus encouraged His followers to be persistent in their requests to their generous heavenly Father.

The three lessons emphasize why and how God's people pray. On the basis of these readings, discuss the following questions:

1. According to the Old Testament lesson, how did God encourage Abraham's intercessions, giving him confidence to continue with them? What does this tell us about the presence of God-fearing people in a community or nation? See Matthew 5:16 and 1 Corinthians 7:13–14.

2. What does the answer that God kept giving to Abraham's intercessions tell us about what He desires? See also Ezekiel 33:11 and 2 Peter 3:8–9.

3. God is merciful and patient (Psalm 103:8, 10). At the same time, He is just. What, therefore, must we acknowledge on the basis of what eventually happened to Sodom? See Hebrews 10:31 and Romans 2:5.

4. What is a greater sin than that of Sodom and Gomorrah? See Matthew 10:14–15 and 11:23.

5. There are certain "mission minded" sects that originated in America that, although they speak highly of Him, do not teach that Jesus Christ is who the Epistle lesson says He is. According to Colossians 2:9, Jesus is unique. How? What confidence does this give to Christians as we pray?

6. When the guilt of our sin overwhelms us so that we are tempted to think that we dare not come to God in prayer, of what are we reminded in Colossians 2:13–15? See also Romans 8:1 and 33–34.

7. In the little parable that Christ tells in the Gospel lesson, how is the borrowing neighbor like Abraham in the Old Testament lesson? How does Jesus encourage us to be like that neighbor and Abraham? How does He equip us to be like them? See Luke 11:13.

8. What words in the "Lord's Prayer" show us that a God-pleasing prayer is the one that mirrors Jesus' own daily life while on earth?

Connect

1. Which of the following counts in our prayer life?

YES	NO	
❏	❏	The arithmetic of prayer (how many prayers we say)
❏	❏	The rhetoric of prayer (how eloquently we pray)
❏	❏	The music of prayer (how melodious our voice)
❏	❏	The seriousness of our prayer (how fervently we pray)
❏	❏	The method of prayer (how orderly our prayer)

   Read Psalm 55:16–17 and 116:2 to verify your answers.
2. A wise Christian once said, "While God is the same everywhere, I am not." She was referring to the fact that she needed to find a special place to pray. Mark 1:35 informs us that Jesus often sought deserted areas in which to pray. What are some of the common obstacles inhibiting you from imitating this action of Christ? What are some possible solutions?

3. For whom do we typically pray? What does the example of Abraham and Jesus remind us regarding whom we should always include in our prayers? See Luke 6:28 and Matthew 5:44. What should we not ask God to do? See Luke 9:54–55.

4. The privilege of prayer becomes misused when we look upon prayer as a sort of wish list or "Aladdin's Lamp." How might such a misunderstanding of prayer occur? What petition in the Lord's Prayer is a guard against such misuse?

5. To what extent does our instant-gratification, performance-oriented culture challenge our confidence in the effectiveness of prayer? What should we, therefore, ask God to grant us? In what way does God's reminder in Isaiah 55:8 supply us with the confidence to keep on asking?

═══ Vision ═══

During This Week

1. A rabbi once said, "Mankind will not perish for want of information, only for want of appreciation." Take time to notice something in a friend, spouse, child, or in your home that is a special gift from God. Thank Him for it.
2. The famous 19th-century English preacher Charles Spurgeon said, "It should be our rule never to see the face of another in the morning before seeing the face of God." Therefore test these words of the psalmist, "But I call to God, and the Lord saves me. Evening, morning and noon I cry out in distress, and He hears my voice" (Psalm 55:16–17).
3. Pray for a specific person you know who either appears to be totally unspiritual or is struggling with a weak faith.

Closing Worship

Sing or pray together "Come, My Soul, with Every Care"(*LW* 433).

Come my soul, with ev'ry care,
Jesus loves to answer prayer;
He Himself bids you to pray,
Therefore will not turn away.

You are coming to your King,
Large petitions with you bring;
For His grace and pow'r are such
None can ever ask too much.

With my burden I begin:
Lord, remove this load of sin;
Let Your blood, for sinners spilt,
Set my conscience free from guilt.

Lord, Your rest to me impart,
Take possession of my heart;
There Your blood-bought right maintain
And without a rival reign.

While I am a pilgrim here,
Let Your love my spirit cheer;
As my guide, my guard, my friend,
Lead me to my journey's end.

Show me what I am to do;
Ev'ry hour my strength renew.
Let me live a life of faith;
Let me die Your people's death.

Scripture Lessons for Next Sunday

Read Ecclesiastes 1:2; 2:18–26; Colossians 3:1–11; and Luke 12:13–21 in preparation for the Eleventh Sunday after Pentecost.

Session 11

The Eleventh Sunday after Pentecost

Ecclesiastes 1:2, 2:18–26; Colossians 3:1–11; Luke 12:13–21

Focus

Theme: *The Right Look in Life*

Law/Gospel Focus

Seduced by the consumerist spirit of our culture, we look to earthly goods for the meaning of life. In His Sacred Word, God gives us the vision to recognize such an outlook as devastating idolatry. Through the presence of Jesus Christ, God holds before our eyes the free gift of everlasting riches in Him.

Objectives

By the enabling power of the Holy Spirit working through God's Word, we will
1. become alert to our culture's hidden persuaders that seduce us into seeking identity, security, and meaning in false gods;
2. learn to appreciate heaven's great riches bestowed on us in Christ;
3. daily turn to God as our only source of lasting happiness.

Opening Worship

Sing or pray together "I Pray You, Dear Lord Jesus" (*LW* 476).
>I pray You, dear Lord Jesus,
>My heart to keep and train
>That I Your holy temple
>From youth to age remain.
>Oh, turn my thoughts forever
>From worldly wisdom's lore;
>If I but learn to know You,
>I shall not want for more.

Introduction

The factory worker on the assembly line, the office worker facing freeway traffic, the householder daily planning the family menu, the farm worker facing another seasonal planting—they all wonder at times whether it is "worth it." Many seek to find life's meaning in accumulating goods and pleasures as they gyrate to the popular song "Material Girl." On the other end of the spectrum are those who see no meaning or joy to life. They nod their heads in agreement to the words in Ernest Hemingway's *Death in the Afternoon*: "There is no remedy for anything in life…. Death is a sovereign remedy for all misfortune."

1. List some of the ways in which the media condition us to accept the philosophy, "The more you have, the happier you'll be." Give examples that prove that this philosophy is untrue.

2. We don't live in a godless age but in one marked by competing gods. Consult Psalm 31:14, then state what it means to have a "god." List two or three such "gods" of present society.

Luther wrote in his Large Catechism, "A god is that to which we look for all good and in which we find refuge in every time of need. To have a god is nothing else than to trust and believe him with our whole heart … the trust and faith of the heart alone make both God and an idol" (*Large Catechism* I, 2).

═══════════════ Inform ═══════════════

Read the following summaries of the Scripture lessons for the Eleventh Sunday in Pentecost.

Ecclesiastes 1:2; 2:18–26—The "Teacher" examines his labors for some lasting profit. He ponders what is left when his life is over. Everything for which he labored becomes the possession of another. He concludes that true wisdom, knowledge, and happiness do not come from human labor but "from the hand of God."

Colossians 3:1–11—Paul first encourages Christians to focus on the gifts Christ has for them, setting their "hearts on things above." They are then challenged to growth in earthly lifestyles that reflect their focus on the heavenly Christ. Thus, they exhibit Christ's great reconciling work.

Luke 12:13–21—While in the midst of encouraging His followers, Jesus is interrupted by a petitioner who demands that Jesus side with him in an inheritance dispute. Seeing a deeper problem, Jesus tells a parable about a rich farmer whose spiritual poverty makes him a "fool."

All three lessons exhort Christians to look beyond present labor and transitory goods to God, the gracious Giver of everlasting gifts.

Discuss the following questions

1. According to the lessons, what reality faces all people? See Ecclesiastes 2:15–16; Luke 12:20.

2. The Old Testament lesson doesn't ask for less hard work or for curtailing the enjoyment of earthly things, but it notes that the purpose of human existence is not found in them. When you think of the things of this life, what perspective gives purpose and enjoyment? See Ecclesiastes 2:24–25 and 1 Timothy 4:4.

3. In what sense was the writer of the Old Testament lesson wiser about life than the man in the parable of the Gospel lesson?

4. The petitioner in the New Testament lesson was guilty of the sin of covetousness. How is this evident in what he demanded of Jesus? Behind the man's petition was the most deadly sin, described in the Epistle lesson. What is that damnable sin? See Colossians 3:5. What word did the man continually use in the parable, indicating his captivity to the damnable sin? See Luke 12:18–19.

5. In Baptism we have put on Jesus' life. Therefore Christians are to relegate to life's dumpster certain "old clothes" (from the "old self"). List some. What is the only motivation for wearing the new spiritual clothes? See Colossians 3:12; Ephesians 4:24 and 5:1–2.

Connect

1. Describe a situation in which you personally experienced a sense of meaninglessness. What rescued you from the pit of despair?

2. According to the Scriptures, what are some of the motivations for our work and efforts? See 1 Thessalonians 2:9; Ephesians 4:28 and Matthew 25:34–40.

3. What is your most valued possession? Who will get it when you die?

4. What do you fear most about death? Though we sorrow over the death of our loved ones, nevertheless, we don't despair over their death or our own coming death. Why? See Psalm 23:4; 2 Corinthians 5:1, 4–8. Jesus teaches us that death is not the opposite of life. What is it, then?

5. Death is a tyrant, the Great Leveler, ridiculous, the enemy, a surprise. Which one of these descriptions flies out from among the rest and pierces your heart? Why?

6. Check the top three priorities for your life right now.
   a. A good time
   b. A good marriage/family
   c. Having nice things
   d. Getting promoted
   e. Being true to myself
   f. Finding self-fulfillment
   g. Making a contribution to humanity
   h. Making a lot of money
   i. Other
   j. Other
      Underline the TOP priority among the three. Does it reflect what the three lessons emphasize? How so or how not?

7. In planning to make a "deposit" in your investment portfolio to become "rich toward God" what might you do this week?

8. It has been said that the totality of our individual lives is represented by the hyphen between the two dates on our tombstone. In one short sentence state what you might want to have written beneath the hyphen to explain the meaning of your life.

Vision

During This Week

1. Pray about and seek the counsel of God's Word in an area of your life where you find difficulty putting off the "old clothes" of sin.
2. Review your wish list of things to be purchased to determine whether you have been seduced into purchasing something as a source of happiness.
3. If you do not have a will, see a lawyer to draw one up. If you have one, consider adding a few statements that will leave to your heirs some spiritual riches.

Closing Worship

Sing or pray together "Who Trusts in God a Strong Abode" (*LW* 414).

> Who trusts in God a strong abode
> In heav'n and earth possesses;
> Who looks in love to Christ above,
> No fear that heart oppresses.
> In You alone, dear Lord, we own
> Sweet hope and consolation,
> Our shield from foes, our balm for woes,
> Our great and sure salvation.

Scripture Lessons for Next Sunday

Read Genesis 15:1–6; Hebrews 11:1–3, 8–16; Luke 12:32–40 in preparation for the Twelfth Sunday after Pentecost.

Session 12

The Twelfth Sunday
after Pentecost

Genesis 15:1–6; Hebrews 11:1–3, 8–16; Luke 12:32–40

Focus

Theme: *The Reward Is Greater than Any Risk*

Law/Gospel Focus

We don't like risks, for we desire to be in complete control at all times; God calls us to acknowledge our limitations. Those who live by faith in the future that God promises and that Christ has made available receive His gracious rewards that surpass any present risks.

Objectives

By the enabling power of the Holy Spirit working through God's Word, we will
1. live our lives as Christian pilgrims, confidently moving into new areas of obedience to God and service to His people;
2. be assured that within every risk God calls us to face, there remains the security of His powerful promises;
3. focus on the Good News in Jesus Christ and His promises that empowers us to move into the unseeable future with certain hope.

Opening Worship

Pray together:
Leader: Doubt sees the obstacles,
Participants: Faith sees the way;
Leader: Doubt sees the blackest night,
Participants: Faith sees the day;
Leader: Doubt dreads to take a step,

Introduction

People who have gained a measure of success in their professions often say that they had to be "risk-takers." The adage "nothing ventured, nothing gained" echoed often in their minds. In the business world, the higher the risk-ratio on a venture, the higher the potential loss, but also the higher the potential gain. Successful risk-takers talk about doing careful research before they act. They take risks based on knowledge.

1. Describe a venture of yours that you thought was risky, but turned out to be rewarding. Why did you try it?

2. Why do some people avoid risks at any cost?

The Bible records the stories of many of God's faithful people who appeared to be foolish risk-takers when seen from any perspective other than that of faith. But the promises that God held before them proved sufficient for them to venture forth into the unseen future with faith.

Inform

Read the following summaries of the Scripture lessons for the Twelfth Sunday after Pentecost.

Genesis 15:1–6—For a third time, God reminds Abram of the promise He had given him—he would not remain childless, and his descendants would be as many as the stars. Trusting in God as his shield and great reward, Abram is pronounced righteous in God's sight.

Hebrews 11:1–3, 8–16—The author describes the characteristics and triumphs of a God-pleasing faith. With confidence it holds to divine realities. Abram and Sarah held to God's promises that were fulfilled in the heavenly city He prepared for them.

Luke 12:32–40—Jesus gives words of encouragement to His followers. Possessing His kingdom they need not seek their treasure in earthly possessions. Using a little story, Jesus exhorts Christians to watchfulness so they may be ready for their reward at the sudden return of the Son of Man.

Discuss the following questions:

1. Consult the Old Testament lesson. Why might Abram be afraid for his life at this time? See Genesis 14:14–17. What two reasons did God give Abram for maintaining courage (15:1)? How are these reasons similar to what Jesus says in the opening words of the Gospel lesson?

2. Troubled with doubts, Abram did the only thing he could do with them. What did he do?

3. Abram was already a rich and famous man. What new blessing did God promise him? See also 15:5 22:17. What were the future implications of that promise? See Romans 4:19–25.

4. What "echo" did God's Word of promise produce in Abram (v. 6a)? See also Rom. 10:14, 17. What did Abraham then receive in God's sight (v. 6b)?

5. By trusting the Eternal One, who gave such wondrous promises, what greater "reward" became Abraham's? See Hebrews 11:10, 16.

6. How does the epistle show us that the attitude of trusting in God's will—rather than our own—has always been the path to salvation?

7. What connection is there between the risk-takers who acted in faith and the reward described in Hebrews 10:35–39? For example, what did Abraham give up? See Genesis 12:1.

8. Hebrews 11:1 and 6 use several verbs to define faith. List them.

9. What is the "object" of faith? See Romans 4:23–25.

10. Is saving faith directed toward the present, toward the future, or both? (See Gal. 2:20 and Heb. 11:16.) Why have you come to this conclusion?

11. More than 380 times the New Testament refers to Christ's glorious, visible return to end the present age of the universe. It will be at an unexpected time. During the present time of waiting,

what does Christ desire of us? (See v. 37.) How do we do this? (See Luke 12:33–37 and Matt. 5:14–16.)

12. What is the relationship between the watchfulness described by Jesus in Luke 12:35–40 and the fears of Jesus' followers addressed in verse 32?

Connect

1. In what area of your life are you longing for certainty?

2. When we fear what lies ahead, what should we remember about God's promise to Abram in the Old Testament lesson?

3. Just when Abram was on the verge of despair over having an heir, God promised descendants too numerous to imagine. What does this promise tell us about God's future blessings to us? See 1 Corinthians 2:9.

4. The Lord credited Abram as "righteous." What affirming words might one use to describe you today because of Christ? See, for example, 1 John 3:1.

5. How has the righteousness you have received through Christ changed your life?

6. As a Christian, in what way have you at times felt like an "alien and stranger on earth"?

Vision

During This Week

1. Many of God's faithful people died without seeing with their earthly eyes all that God had promised, yet they never lost their vision of "a better country—a heavenly one." When you feel defeated because an appeal to God is not yet fulfilled, ask Him for the gift of patience and a clearer fix on what is already yours in Christ.
2. Phone an individual you know who needs to have someone "reach out and touch" him or her with a word that personalizes the promises of God. Risk rejection.
3. Seek God's guidance through Scripture regarding the present securities that you need to leave behind on your journey of faith.

Closing Worship

Sing or pray together "My Faith Looks Trustingly" (*LW* 378).

My faith looks trustingly
To Christ of Calvary,
My Savior true!
Lord, hear me while I pray,
Take all my guilt away,
Strengthen in ev'ry way
My love for You!

May Your rich grace impart
Strength to my fainting heart,
My zeal inspire;

As You have died for me,
My love, adoringly,
Pure, warm, and changeless be,
A living fire!

While life's dark maze I tread
And griefs around me spread,
Oh, be my guide;
Make darkness turn to day,
Wipe sorrow's tears away,
Nor let me ever stray
From You aside.

When ends life's transient dream,
When death's cold, sullen stream
Rolls over me,
Blest Savior, then in love
Fear and distrust remove;
Oh, bear me safe above,
Redeemed and free!

Scripture Lessons for Next Sunday

Read Jeremiah 23:23–29; Hebrews 12:1–13; and Luke 12:49–53 in preparation for the Thirteenth Sunday after Pentecost.

Session 13

The Thirteenth Sunday after Pentecost

Jeremiah 23:23–29; Hebrews 12:1–13; Luke 12:49–53

Focus

Theme: *The Truth and Its Consequences*

Law/Gospel Focus

We are prone to believe lies regarding the deceptive power of sin and to misunderstand the purpose of God's disciplining His children. In all our struggles and suffering, God remains our caring Father, who through Christ has made us the beloved members of His family.

Objectives

As we study God's Word, through the enlightening power of the Holy Spirit, we will
1. be alert to false prophets who misrepresent God's Word, accommodating it to the false gods of their age;
2. be vigorous in persevering against sin in us and around us;
3. be strengthened in the conviction that the peace Christ has established between God and us is the truth that will overcome any suffering that is the consequence of Christian witness.

Opening Worship

Pray together:

Leader: Dear Heavenly Father, hold clearly before our eyes
Participants: The glorious vision of Your sustaining presence.
Leader: Dear Christ, Author and Perfecter of our faith,
Participants: Accompany us with Your forgiveness, that we may persevere in the race You set before us.
Leader: O Holy Spirit, Creator of life and holiness in us,

Introduction

"Nothin' worth somethin' costs nothin'." Olympic athletes going for the gold realize that other things in life take second place to the rigorous training for international competition. They know from experience that there is no gain without some pain. By the time the Olympic event occurs, they have invested the time and effort and can tell whether they are ready for the contest or not.

1. List several professions in which a person tries to predict the future?

2. Why do people read their horoscope?

3. What are some of the things that people like to be told, even when they know what is being said is most likely untrue? Why?

4. What changes in lifestyle are necessary in order to diet? to maintain your weight after dieting?

Inform

Read the following summaries of the Scripture lessons for the Thirteenth Sunday after Pentecost.

Jeremiah 23:23–29—The prophet alerts God's people to the dangers presented by spiritual leaders who stop resisting an evil culture by not expressing disapproval of its sinful behavior. God's people, however, are to speak His Word faithfully and in so doing, destroy falsehood.

Hebrews 12:1–13—The Christian life is pictured as a race in which all Christians are running. Christians are exhorted to run the race with patience and resolve. By keeping their eyes on Jesus, who put them into the race, they will be able to finish it successfully. The discipline endured along the way, even if unpleasant, only serves to make them stronger runners.

Luke 12:49–53—Jesus expresses His desire to complete His self-sacrificing mission—to accomplish redemption for all people. He alerts His followers to the divisions that will occur because of their loyalty to Him.

1. According to the Old Testament lesson, what is a characteristic of a false prophet? See Jeremiah 23:27 and 32; also Deuteronomy 13:1–5. What false image of God do false prophets project (Jeremiah 23:23–24)?

2. Has God used dreams to reveal His will? See Genesis 28:12 and Matthew 1:20. But what do false prophets do? (Jeremiah 23:26, 32) Were there also false prophets in New Testament times? In present times? See 2 Thessalonians 2:9–12; 1 Timothy 4:1–2; 2 Timothy 4:3–4.

3. According to the epistle, what often happens to Christians in their faith "marathon" (Hebrews 12:12)? What keeps Christians in the race?

4. According to the epistle lesson, what does the runner do to prepare himself for staying on the course (v. 1)?

5. According to the epistle, what sometimes distorts human methods of discipline?

6. While the truth is that God must discipline us, what are the intended consequences of our heavenly Father's discipline?

7. In the Gospel lesson, Jesus, like John the Baptizer, uses the Old Testament image of fire. What does it symbolize? See John 5:27 and Luke 3:16–17. What coming act of Jesus in Jerusalem would be His "baptism"?

8. How does following Jesus result in division? How does this relate to Luke 12:31–34? Jesus' words came out of His own experience with earthly families. What do we learn about this in John 7:3–5?

Connect

1. What obstacles in our path may cause us to stumble along the way to our heavenly goal? What perspective must we struggle to maintain if we are to remain in the race? See Hebrews 12:11–13; consult also 1 Corinthians 11:32 and 2 Corinthians 12:7.

2. Describe how your life has grown spiritually through suffering, or how you have been spiritually enriched by some Christian's witness in the midst of suffering.

3. Can you recall anything your pastor said in a sermon that may have made you uncomfortable, but proved to be the necessary, loving discipline that either you or the congregation needed to hear?

4. What divisive subjects do you consider unfit for discussion when you get together with family or friends? Has Christ brought your family and friends division or peace? Why?

5. How can you tell if it is spiritual convictions—or the way you express them—that strain a relationship? See 1 Peter 3:15.

Vision

During This Week

1. Think of opportunities in which, through God's empowerment, you can challenge the status quo among your peers. Your goal is to apply God's will for their lives in a very practical and visible way.

2. With a friend or acquaintance who is not a member of your denomination, discuss in a nonthreatening way some doctrinal differences that exist between you. Be sure to emphasize that your mutual love for Christ is the reason you seek to retain His teachings in their fullness and purity.
3. Watch a TV soap. Analyze what views regarding life's goals are presented as acceptable, even though they are at odds with what the Bible says.

Closing Worship

Sing "Fight the Good Fight" (*LW* 299).

> Fight the good fight with all your might;
> Christ is your strength, and Christ your right.
> Lay hold on life, and it shall be
> Your joy and crown eternally.
>
> Run the straight race through God's good grace;
> Lift up your eyes, and seek His face.
> Life with its way before us lies;
> Christ is the path, and Christ the prize.
>
> Cast care aside, lean on your guide;
> His boundless mercy will provide.
> Trust, and enduring faith shall prove
> Christ is your life and Christ your love.
>
> Faint not nor fear, His arms are near;
> He changes not who holds you dear;
> Only believe, and you will see
> That Christ is all eternally.

Scripture Lessons for Next Sunday

Read Isaiah 66:18–23; Hebrews 12:18–24; and Luke 13:22–30 in preparation for the Fourteenth Sunday after Pentecost.

Session 14

The Fourteenth Sunday after Pentecost

Isaiah 66:18–23; Hebrews 12:18–24; Luke 13:22–30

Focus

Theme: *Life's Most Important Question*

Law/Gospel Focus

Often we hide from, ignore, or disregard the most important thing in life—our personal relationship to God and His call to repentance and faith in Jesus Christ. Because Christ redeemed the world through His blood shed on the cross, He desires and has made possible for each individual a personal relationship with God. Through the proclamation of the Gospel the Holy Spirit works to create and to sustain saving faith so that each individual might partake of the blessings of salvation enjoyed by the saints in glory.

Objectives

By the enabling power of the Holy Spirit working through God's Word, we will
1. confess that our relationship to God our Creator and Redeemer is not always first in our lives;
2. be assured that Christ, through His cross, has obtained for all people access to the eternal assembly of God's blessed;
3. with joy acknowledge Christ's creation of a vast community of the redeemed into which He has made each of us members through His blood.

Opening Worship

Read this responsive reading, taken from "Glory Be to Jesus" (*LW* 98).
Leader: Glory be to Jesus, Who in bitter pains,
Participants: Poured for me the lifeblood from His sacred veins.
Leader: Abel's blood for vengeance pleaded to the skies,
Participants: But the blood of Jesus for our pardon cries.

Introduction

Near the beginning of a new year, many magazines carry articles dealing with what's in and what's out in fashion, food, and even people. The lists often include what words are politically correct and which are not. The lists even show that certain questions are considered fitting to ask, such as, "Is this product environmentally safe?"

1. Is Christianity considered in or out in our society? What evidence do you have for your answer?

2. Is Christianity in or out in your life? What evidence can you provide?

At times most of us must confess that our words, actions, and attitudes indicate that Christianity is out. Fortunately, God in His love and mercy continues to offer His forgiveness to us through Jesus and provides us through His means—Word and Sacrament—the faith-strengthening power to demonstrate through our words, actions, and attitude that Christianity is "in."

═══════════ Inform ═══════════

Read the following summaries of the Scripture lessons for the Fourteenth Sunday after Pentecost.

Isaiah 66:18–23—Through the prophet Isaiah, God foretells Israel's return to Jerusalem and the promised land. Israel's return is a prophetic symbol of a worldwide redemption for all people, including those (the Gentiles) who once did not know the way to the true God and His worship.

Hebrews 12:18–24—The lesson reaches a climax in a section that portrays the surpassing supremacy and attractiveness of the heavenly Jerusalem and the new testament established by Jesus' blood.

Luke 13:22–30—As Jesus made His way to Jerusalem, where He would be crucified, someone asked Him whether only a few people would be His followers. Jesus addressed the crowd regarding the urgency of entering the narrow door to the heavenly feast before the door is closed and they will never be allowed to enter. He does tell them that many people will come from all directions to feast in God's kingdom.

Answer the following questions:

1. According to the Old Testament lesson, when God encouraged the Jews to look beyond their national boundaries, what sin did He want them to overcome? (see also Romans 3:29; Matthew 28:19; Acts 1:8)

2. Often God's people become despondent because they realize the low level of spirituality among so many people in the world. What hope is included in Isaiah 66:22–23? See also Philippians 2:9–11 and Revelation 11:15.

3. What verse in the Isaiah prophecy relates to Jesus' prophecy in Luke 13:29?

4. What indication is there in the prophecy that after Judgment Day there is a wonderful new world awaiting God's people? See also 2 Peter 3:13 and Revelation 21:1.

5. In the Epistle lesson, what two mountains are contrasted? What are the two different reactions they produce from people?

6. What is the "better word" (Hebrews 12:24) in contrast to "no further word" (v. 19)? See also John 1:17 and Romans 5:5.

7. What did Jesus' self-sacrifice establish between God and us? How does He come today to give the blessings won by His one-time sacrifice? See Matthew 26:26–29.

8. In the Gospel lesson, as Jesus traveled to Jerusalem, what destiny was on His mind?

9. Rather than answering the inquirer's question about other people, how did Jesus redirect the concern?

10. Study the historical context of this lesson to discover who were some of the people who would find themselves outside the shut door. See also Luke 11:23, 37–53; 12:9, 21, 45–46.

Connect

1. How do you know whether you are among those "inside" or "outside" the Kingdom? See Luke 10:20 and John 3:16–18. What is the entrance key? See Luke 12:32 and Ephesians 2:4–8.

2. God desires that all people be "in" His heavenly kingdom. What words, actions, and attitudes might you demonstrate to indicate that Christianity is "in" your life?

3. How might the Holy Spirit work through these words, actions, and attitudes so that others outside the "door" desire to get in?

Vision

During This Week

1. If there is a spiritual problem that hinders your enjoyment of the comfort Christ gives, set up an appointment with your pastor to discuss it.
2. Pray for a specific person you know who does not confess Jesus as Lord and Savior. Pray that the Spirit might use you to witness boldly your faith to this person.
3. Seek guidance from God's Word about how you can be an instrument in His hands for a wider gathering of people into the city of God.

Closing Worship

Sing or pray together stanza 3 of "Seek Where You May to Find a Way" (*LW* 358).

> Seek Him alone,
> Do not postpone;
> Let Him your soul deliver.
> All you who thirst,
> Go to Him first
> Whose grace flows like a river.
> Seek Him indeed
> In ev'ry need;
> He will impart
> To ev'ry heart
> The fullness of His treasure.

Scripture Lessons for Next Sunday

Read in preparation for the Fifteenth Sunday after Pentecost Proverbs 25:6–7; Hebrews 13:1–8; and Luke 14:1, 7–14.

Session 15

The Fifteenth Sunday after Pentecost

Proverbs 25:6–7; Hebrews 13:1–8; Luke 14:1, 7–14

Focus

Theme: *The Characteristic of True Greatness*

Law/Gospel Focus

Our self-centeredness keeps us from realistically evaluating ourselves, both as we stand in the presence of others and in the presence of God. Despite the way sin blinds and cripples us, Christ graciously invites us to be His honored guests at God's table.

Objectives

By the enabling power of the Holy Spirit working through God's Word we will

1. acknowledge that before God we are poor in spirit, dependent on His giving us places of honor;
2. seek, in the spirit of Christ's self-giving, to serve the weak and lowly;
3. be content with God's gifts to us because of Christ's continuing presence among us.

Opening Worship

Leader:	Let us pray that we may learn from Jesus' words:
Participants:	Dear Heavenly Father, draw us to Him.
Leader:	That all Christians may be convinced that humility is a form of strength, and that it opens doors that would otherwise remain closed;
Participants:	Lord Jesus, help us to learn from Your example.
Leader:	That in all our dealings we may turn from pride and arrogance;
Participants:	Holy Spirit empower us.
ALL:	Amen.

Introduction

Students are graded, teachers are evaluated, employer and employee alike are assessed. How are we better than someone else? Who is the best? Various types of advice are offered on how to advance ourselves successfully. We hear expressions such as, "If you don't look out for yourself, no one else will." "You've gotta play the game!" "It's not what you know, but who you know." "Get them before they get you." In the ancient Greco-Roman world as well as in today's competitive world, exalting the virtue of humility seems to make as much sense as praising a diet book to a starving man. Yet the "Good Book" of God's Word does exalt humility.

1. In what way is humility often mistaken for weakness, and meekness equated with being mousey?

2. In what way does the desire to dominate, to always be number 1, feed the flame of personal unrest and family disunity?

===== Inform =====

Read the following summaries of the Scripture lessons for the Fifteenth Sunday after Pentecost.

Proverbs 25:6–7—The sage advises the reader not to try assigning himself a prominent place in the presence of a superior. To do so results in being unworthy to occupy a position reserved for the honored.

Hebrews 13:1–8—The writer gives concluding exhortations to the Christian community regarding those to whom they should extend brotherly love and hospitality. Because Christians have the ever-present help of the changeless Christ, they can extend help to the homeless, the imprisoned, and those struggling to maintain their marriage commitment.

Luke 14:1, 7–14—At a Sabbath Day dinner in the home of a Pharisee, Jesus was being scrutinized by the guests. Having observed how the guests all sought the seats of honor, Jesus told a parable. Then He spoke directly to the host about whom he should invite to feast with him.

Answer the following questions.

1. The words of the Old Testament lesson appear not to be spiritual, just social etiquette. Yet a major theological premise underlies this advice. What is it? See Proverbs 15:33 and 24:21.

2. A celebration meal, such as at a wedding, is an image Jesus used often. To what does he compare such a celebration? See Matthew 22:2; 26:27–29; Revelation 19:7.

3. What attitude is praised in the Old Testament lesson and the Gospel lesson? How does this element serve to unite the two lessons?

4. According to the Gospel lesson, what activity of the dinner guests attracts Jesus' attention? How does Jesus' view of honor vary from that held by many of His contemporaries? See Mark 10:42–45. How does His advice to the host exemplify His own activity? See Luke 15:1 and 18:35–43.

5. What is the principle that God applies in dealing with people (Luke 14:11)? See also Luke 1:46–49, 51–53; Ephesians 2:8–9.

6. According to the Epistle lesson, in what ways should Christians exhibit brotherly love? What help is offered for those who strive to fulfill these exhortations (Hebrews 13:6, 8).

7. How are we to regard our spiritual leaders (vv. 7 and 17)? Why?

8. Money is a necessary means of exchange in complex societies. Jesus said, "The laborer is worthy of his hire." It is not money that produces discontent, but what (v. 5)? What kind of confidence is an antidote for the disease of discontent (see vv. 5, 6, 8)?

=============================== **Connect** ===============================

1. How do such things as social expectations and status get in the way of extending love and acceptance to others in your family? your workplace?

2. Comment on the following statement. Princeton University researcher Robert Wuthnow writes, "We do not feel compelled to give up any of our material desires; only to put them in perspective" ("Pious Materialism: How Americans View Faith and Money," copyright 1994 Christian Century Foundation. Reprinted by permission from the March 3, 1994, issue of *The Christian Century.*)

3. Do you agree or disagree with the following statements.
    a. I think a lot about money and finances.
    b. I wish I had more money.
    c. I feel having more money would make me feel better about myself.
    d. I support the position that it is wrong to want a lot of money.
    e. I make large purchases (e.g., a car) that best fit my spiritual values.
Pick the statement with which you most agree and most disagree. Why your strong agreement? disagreement?

Vision

During This Week

1. Do for someone else a task that you once thought unworthy of your time or effort. Think of it now as a way to acknowledge your appreciation of the person for whom you do it.
2. Make a mental note of how many times a day you find yourself tempted to compare what you have or don't have with another.
3. Start the day with a prayer of thanksgiving to God for the gift of physical life and eternal life.
4. Post in a prominent place Paul's secret recipe of contentment recorded in Philippians 4:11–13.

Closing Worship

Sing or pray together the first four stanzas of "What God Ordains Is Always Good" (*LW* 422).

> What God ordains is always good:
> His will is just and holy.
> As He directs my life for me,
> I follow meek and lowly.
> My God indeed
> In ev'ry need
> Knows well how He will shield me;
> To Him, then, I will yield me.
>
> What God ordains is always good:
> He never will deceive me.
> He leads me in His own right way,
> And never will He leave me.
> I take content
> What He has sent;
> His hand that sends me sadness
> Will turn my tears to gladness.
>
> What God ordains is always good:
> His loving thought attends me;

No poison can be in the cup
That my physician sends me.
My God is true;
Each morning new
I trust His grace unending,
My life to Him commending.

What God ordains is always good:
He is my friend and father;
He suffers naught to do me harm
Though many storms may gather.
Now I may know
Both joy and woe;
Someday I shall see clearly
That He has loved me dearly.

Scripture Lessons for Next Sunday

Read Proverbs 9:8–12; Philemon 1–21; and Luke 14:25–33 in preparation for the Sixteenth Sunday after Pentecost.